Martin Plowman has been a mediator for fifteen years, and has successfully mediated over a thousand cases. He is the only mediator to have been ranked in the top three mediators in the United Kingdom by the independent National Mediator Database in each of the past ten years. He is a regular speaker on mediation and negotiation, and has taught 'Zen and the Art of Mediation' at the University of East Anglia. He is a solicitor, and before qualifying as a mediator was Head of the Litigation Department at a large provincial solicitors' firm. He is also a student of Zen.

Zen and the Art of Mediation

Zen and the Art of Mediation

Martin Plowman
Solicitor
Mediator
Norwich City FC Season Ticket Holder

Law Brief Publishing

© Martin Plowman

All rights reserved. No part of this publication may be reproduced, stored in a retrieval system, or transmitted, in any form or by any means, electronic, mechanical, photocopying, recording or otherwise, without the prior permission of the publisher.

Cover image © iStockphoto.com/ansonsaw

The information in this book was believed to be correct at the time of writing. All content is for information purposes only and is not intended as legal advice. No liability is accepted by either the publisher or author for any errors or omissions (whether negligent or not) that it may contain. Professional advice should always be obtained before applying any information to particular circumstances. In order too protect confidentiality, all names, facts and details in this book have been fictionalised.

Published 2019 by Law Brief Publishing, an imprint of Law Brief Publishing Ltd
30 The Parks
Minehead
Somerset
TA24 8BT

www.lawbriefpublishing.com

Paperback: 978-1-912687-33-6

CONTENTS

Introduction	The Mediator and the Seventeen Camels	1
	Something magical	3
	Isn't all this Zen stuff a bit freaky?	6
	And a disclaimer	8
Chapter One	My greatest mediation teacher	11
Chapter Two	The First Noble Truth	27
	The Buddha and the man with 83 problems	30
	Recognition and affirmation	33
	Empathy	38
Chapter Three	The Second Noble Truth	49
	Language and cinders	51
	But what about Morality?	54
	Zazen: stilling the mental narrative?	58
Chapter Four	The Third Noble Truth	63
	A slap in the face with a wet fish	64
	The opening joint session	71
	A memo to barristers and mediation advocates	78
	What about Transformative Mediation?	82
	Keeping an open mind	86
Chapter Five	Not always so	89
	Schrödinger's cat and probability waves	91
	Risk in litigation	93
	Reframing	96
	A fanfare for the common lawyer	98
	Risk aversion and loss Aversion	104

Chapter Six	A mediation	115
	Something magical (2)	137
	The art of evaluating risk	146
	Zen Mediation	149
Chapter Seven	The Fourth Noble Truth	151
	The goalless goal	154
Appendix	Top Ten Mistakes To Avoid for Mediators	159
Acknowledgments		163

INTRODUCTION

The Mediator and the Seventeen Camels

May I tell you a story?

It may not be literally true. But like all the best stories, it's a bridge to the truth....

> "Once upon a time, a Mediator was riding through the endless wastes of the desert on his camel. The Mediator had been riding for a long time and as he scanned the sea of sand that surrounded him, he was pleased to see the palm trees of an oasis on the horizon. He turned his trusty camel towards the oasis.
>
> But as the Mediator neared the oasis he realised that all was not well. Raised voices drifted across the sands towards him, and he caught the unmistakable glint of sunlight on drawn swords. By the time the Mediator arrived in the oasis it was apparent that a full-blown conflict was about to break out. Anxious to help (or, perhaps, seeing the opportunity for an unexpected bit of business) the Mediator enquired as to what the problem might be.
>
> The sad story was soon told. An old, and important member of the tribe had died. He had provided for the distribution of his worldly goods in his will, and, as was common in those days, in that part of the world, he had divided his goods between his three sons, giving the most to the eldest, and least to the youngest. The eldest son was to receive one half of the estate, the middle son was to receive one third of the estate and the youngest son was to receive one ninth of the estate. That in itself would not have triggered a conflict, for the principle was not unusual, but the difficulty lay in the fact that the man's estate consisted entirely of seventeen camels.
>
> In a part of the world where wealth was measured in camels this was a significant number. The difficulty, however, was that sev-

enteen is a number that can be divided neither by two, to give the eldest son a half, nor by a third nor a ninth to give the next two sons their proper shares. Hence the impending conflict. The eldest son, not unnaturally, felt that as the eldest he should have a bit more, but his younger brothers, again understandably, felt that as their older brother was already receiving the most it was he who should give something up. The only compromise that had been suggested was to kill all seventeen camels, to weigh the meat, and then to divide the estate that way. Unfortunately, whilst it was superficially attractive this solution was, in the searing heat of the desert, and before the age of the deep freeze, simply not practicable. So swords had been drawn, and the members of the family were about to fall upon each other, when the unexpected chance that a Mediator should suddenly appear out of the desert gave them a glimmer of hope, and they enquired of the Mediator whether he could help.

A fee was negotiated, and paid by each of the brothers out of their own assets, and the Mediator then said "I shall give you my camel". The Mediator's suggestion provoked amazement, with some asking how that was supposed to help, and others questioning the Mediator's sanity. The Mediator went on to explain:

"Now you have eighteen camels. Eighteen is divisible by two, so the eldest son can have nine camels. Eighteen is divisible by three, so the middle son can have six camels and eighteen is divisible by nine, so the youngest son can have two camels.

Satisfied, and overjoyed to have avoided a conflict, each of the sons took his camels and returned to his tent. And best of all, since nine plus six plus two comes to seventeen, the Mediator's own camel was left over and the Mediator was able to climb back onto his trusty camel and to resume his voyage across the desert".

Something magical

This is a book about something magical.

Magical because, as the story of the Mediator and the Seventeen Camels shows, the intervention of an independent mediator can resolve disputes where no resolution seems possible[1].

Magical because mediation can change lives and transform people. Yes, really. A few weeks ago I mediated an inheritance claim in Birmingham. The mediation almost failed half an hour before it was due to start. The dispute was between two sisters, and the previous evening one had sent an email round her family describing the other as "the bitch-cow from hell". On the morning of the mediation one sister had caught a glimpse of the bitch-cow from hell arriving at the mediation venue, with the result that each refused even to enter a building containing the other. Not promising, you may think. But, eight hours later, after a mediation conducted partly in solicitors' offices and partly in Starbucks[2], we had a settlement, and the sisters were embracing each other, the "bitch-cow from hell" transformed into a "dear lost sister".

In my book, that's more magical than transforming a bunch of flowers into a white rabbit any day. So, yes, this is a book about something magical. This is a book about the art of mediation.

You'll have worked that out from the title, of course. I am what we in the UK call a "commercial mediator", so "commercial mediation" is what I know about. "Commercial mediation", as the name suggests, includes business disputes, but in practice the term also seems to extend to a range of other quarrels that don't really have anything to do with the commercial world: inheritance disputes, neighbour disputes, and disputes between separating couples over who owns what shares in

---

1 Yes, I know. The maths in the will was up the spout. One half plus one third plus one ninth doesn't add up to a whole camel, or a whole anything else. But, the point still stands. The intervention of an independent mediator can resolve disputes where no resolution seems possible. Which is magic of a kind.

2 Other coffee shops are available.

property, for example. I think the term "commercial" is really being used here to distinguish the kind of mediation that I do from dispute resolution in a family context, such as when a marriage or relationship has broken down, or mediation within a workplace or a community where, again, a relationship breakdown is often very much the issue. I'm guessing, though, that much of what I do in a "commercial" mediation applies to mediation in any situation: within a family, in the workplace, or in a divided community. So hopefully you'll find something in this book for you whether you're a commercial mediator, another kind of mediator, or whether you're simply someone whose everyday existence involves resolving disputes.

When I talk about mediation, by the way, that's mediation with one "t". Not medi*t*ation, which has an extra "t". Mediation, with only the one "t", is where a neutral third party – the mediator – helps the parties to a dispute come to a resolution. That's what I do. Medi*t*ation, with the extra "t", is a practice of silent contemplation practised in Zen Buddhism (and elsewhere). And that's also what I do.

If you are a budding mediator and were simply looking for a manual containing mediation techniques, then I'm afraid that this isn't quite that book. Sorry about that. There's plenty of books out there on mediation technique. Some of them are even written by people who know something about mediation. But if that were what you were after, don't despair. Firstly, in the course of this book we'll touch on plenty of the techniques that I've found to be effective in my mediation work, so you'll certainly be picking up some mediation techniques as we go along. And secondly, technique isn't the be-all and the end-all in mediation. Sure, technique has its place. Technique is important. And, yes, you can learn and deploy mediation techniques without them coming, as it were, from your heart. And they'll have some effect. But here's the thing: in my experience mediation techniques work *better* when they do come from the heart. And that's what this book is about. About the place the techniques come from. Technique is ultimately just about *how* we do something. This book is about *why* we'd want to do it in the first place. Because if you understand why you might want to use a particular technique, and where that technique is going, well, then, that will empower your mediation technique because it will come from the heart. In fact, if you really, really get what's going on in a mediation, you'll probably find that mediation technique comes naturally to you and you won't even need a book on technique, the whole technique, and nothing but the technique.

And if the reference to Zen in the title drew you to this book, and you were expecting a Zen manual then, again, I'm sorry. This isn't that book either. There are plenty of books claiming to be Zen manuals, or just with random references to Zen in the title out there, too. A proportion of them even have something to do with Zen. But if Zen tips were what you were after, then you'll be pleased to hear that, although this is most definitely not a Zen manual, it is nevertheless a book about Zen, or at any rate, a book about how my own Zen practice, and the way of looking at the world that comes with Zen practice, has informed and even empowered my work as a mediator.

Having said that, I need to make something clear here. When he heard that I was writing a book on Zen and the Art of Mediation a friend looked at me with a new respect and said that he didn't know that I was a Zen Master. Well, er, that would be because I'm not a Zen Master. My wife Karen and I share our home with a fat cat called Zazen. I think she may be a Zen Master. The cat, not Karen, who is neither fat nor a Zen Master. But I'm certainly no Zen Master. I'm not a Zen teacher. I'm just a student of Zen. And always will be. That's all. Whether the fact that I've mediated over a thousand disputes enables me to speak with any degree of authority on mediation, I leave to you, dear reader. Authority is very much in the eye of the beholder. But on matters Zen I definitely don't have or even claim any authority. If you want an authoritative teaching on a Zen issue, find a Zen teacher. As I said, this is simply a book about how this mediator's Zen practice has informed and empowered his mediation work.

And please, don't get me wrong. I'm not saying that to be an effective mediator you have to be a Zen Buddhist. Not at all. It's just that I have found that a mediator is most effective when they give of themselves. If your thing were, say, ballroom dancing, I'd guess that there would be things that you might bring to your mediation practice from ballroom dancing. There may be a book waiting to be written on Ballroom Dancing and the Art of Mediation. If you think that there is, go ahead and write it: I'll split the royalties with you. But I don't do ballroom dancing (though I'd quite like to) whereas I do practise Zen, and as a result it is my Zen practice that has informed and empowered my mediation work.

So, this is a book about Zen and the art of mediation.

Isn't all this Zen stuff a bit freaky?

When I talk about Zen and Mediation in the same sentence, I can't help noticing that sometimes the people I'm talking to are a little uneasy. Perhaps they are serious professional people who view mediation – rightly – as a serious professional business, and they ask themselves whether Zen isn't just a bit, well, a bit freaky? Won't it involve incense, or chanting, or drugs? Or perhaps they come to mediation with (or even because of) a religious faith, which faith involves a set of beliefs – about the creator of the universe, about our relationship to said creator, about the purpose of life, and so on. Heavy stuff. And they worry that Zen Buddhism may represent a conflicting system of beliefs, and they are uneasy that by talking about Zen I'm pushing heresy at them. Maybe people are worried that if they let their guard down then in no time I'll have them burning incense, chanting Om Mane Padme Hum, and worshipping statues of the Buddha. Fair enough. I get that.

If you're in any of these categories, this is for you. I appreciate, of course, that if you're in any of these categories, the title of this book has probably put you off already, and so it's most likely that I'm talking to myself here. But just on the off chance that there is someone out there reading this who has these concerns, this is for you. If Zen doesn't strike you as freaky, or if it does but you're cool with the freakiness, or if your faith just isn't troubled by the mention of Zen, then you can skip this section. Or not, as you like. It's your book (assuming you've bought it and aren't just reading it in the bookshop, in which case go and buy it first) and you can read whichever bits you like.

For anyone who's still with me, let me try to clear up a couple of common misunderstandings.

First, Zen Buddhists do not hold the Buddha to be God. The Buddha expressly said that he wasn't any kind of deity. The title "Buddha" just means "enlightened person" and doesn't imply any kind of claim to divinity.

The historical Buddha is said to have been a guy called Siddhartha Gautama. It is claimed that he lived in what is now Nepal or northern India about 2,500 years ago. Did he really exist? I don't know. If he did exist, are the stories about him all historical fact? Again, I don't know. I'd be surprised if they were all factually true. Does it matter? Nope. Not a jot. Zen doesn't depend on whether the Buddha existed, or whether the stories about him are factually true at all.

One of those stories tells of the folk who lived in a place called Kalama. Kalama lay at a crossroads and so a fair bit of traffic came their way. Including plenty of religious teachers. The good people of Kalama noticed something about the religious teachers. Each of them claimed that they, and they alone, taught the truth. Which may sound familiar to you. And one day the Buddha came to Kalama. So the people there said to him "We gather that you're a teacher. Well, we have a problem with teachers. They all claim to be teaching the only truth, and we don't know which one to believe. Which one should we believe?" I'm guessing they expected the Buddha to reply "D'oh! You believe me, of course!" But instead the Buddha said something like this: "D'oh! Believe none of them. Don't believe anyone just because they claim to tell the truth. Test what anyone tells you against your own experience. Question it. Probe it. And if you find it to be true, then hold it to be the truth, but because you have found it to be true, not because somebody else told you it was the truth. And most of all, don't believe a word I say just because I say it".

Did that really happen? I don't know. But you get the point of the story. Zen Buddhism isn't a belief system at all. It's about seeing for yourself. The word "Zen" translates simply as "meditation". Zen is meditation, and to practice Zen is to sit quietly and look at the world. To really look at it. To look at what's actually there, not to take on trust any of the stories that we tell ourselves about it. That's all. And when you think about it, there's really nothing freaky about looking at the world as it actually is.

And when you look at the world as it actually is, you might decide that everything I say about Zen, and all the stories about the Buddha and Zen Masters in this book, are total rubbish. Not a problem. If you've paid for this book, then you're allowed to think whatever you want about it. Actually, you're allowed to think whatever you want about the book whether or not you've paid for it.

But whilst thinking all the Zen stuff in this book is rubbish is fine, and very much in line with what the Buddha told the folks at Kalama, it would be a pity. I hope there will be things in this book that do ring true to you, and that you can embrace. Because if there are, and if you can embrace the attitude that comes with them, or, even better, recognise that attitude already present in yourself, I think that will make you a better mediator or dispute resolver. Like I say, mediation technique works better when it comes from the heart.

Either way, nothing in this book is an attempt to persuade anyone who holds any faith to abandon it. And it won't be freaky, and we won't burn any incense, and there will definitely be no chanting. That's a promise.

And a Disclaimer

Well, what did you expect? At the end of the day, a book about mediation is a law book, isn't it? Law books have to have a disclaimer, otherwise they're not proper law books.

Anyhow, this is important. Mediations are confidential. I owe a duty of confidentiality to everyone I've ever mediated. And I take that duty very, very seriously. One of the reasons why people instruct a mediator is precisely because they trust the mediator to sort out their disputes in confidence. I respect that trust. Totally.

The same applies to the identities of clients of mine from my days as a solicitor. I owe them a duty of confidentiality too.

It's a bit more of a moot point as to whether I owe a duty of confidentiality to the lawyers whose clients' cases I've mediated. There are different opinions amongst mediators about that. My view is that I do owe them a duty of confidentiality. But, even if I didn't, as far as I'm concerned, if I identified a lawyer in connection with a particular mediation, that would be one step closer to enabling the client who retained that lawyer to be identified. And I'm not prepared to go even one step down that route. So, as far as I'm concerned, lawyers' identities are confidential too.

And then, in chapter one, I've written about my greatest mediation teacher: a guy who mediated a case of mine back when I was a solicitor. I'm pretty sure I don't owe him a duty of confidentiality. But if I said anything that enabled him to be identified then, again, that might be one step down the line to identifying the client I was representing. So, he gets anonymity too.

Over and above the issue of anonymity, I feel slightly ambivalent about the practice of mediators telling what are often referred to as "war stories" about cases they've mediated, usually to illustrate how clever they were. On the one hand, you'll have gathered already that I think mediation is a really, really good thing, and that if anything the world needs more, not less mediation. Which means that it's important that mediators can share their experiences, suitably anonymised of course, because that's how we'll all learn and become better mediators. Which would be a good thing. On the other hand, the cases that people entrusted to me to mediate were all, well, *theirs*. Sensitive. Personal. Private. And displaying those cases to the world, even anonymised, and even for the best of motives to educate and assist other mediators, litigators and negotiators, nevertheless wouldn't feel quite right. It would be a bit like displaying the contents of someone's underwear draw to the world.

All of which means that, first, every detail that I've written about has been changed to make it impossible to identify either the individuals (clients or lawyers) involved or the mediation involved. What the dispute was about, locations, nationalities, genders, inside leg measurements, all of them: changed, all utterly changed. As a result, if there's anyone out there who reads anything in this book and thinks "That sounds like my case", or "That sounds like me", well, if it sounds like your case, or if it sounds like you, then it isn't your case, and it isn't you. Ok? And then, I've stitched together and cut and pasted things that happened in different mediations, and added a dose of my own imagination from time to time, so that I'm never even writing about one particular, actual, mediation, even with names and identifying details changed.

Does that mean that this book is ultimately a work of fiction? Well, maybe. Perhaps that's up to you to decide. Not one mediation happened just exactly in the way I've told it in this book, so I guess you could say it's all made up. But I don't think of this book as fiction. Just as I've checked and re-checked every mediation story I've told and everyone of the dramatis personae that I've referred to in order to make sure that no potentially identifying details remain, I've also checked and re-checked to make sure that every example I give, every story I tell, actually happened. Just not like that. Not in that location. Not with someone like the person I've described. Not in a mediation about that issue. And where I've stitched together bits from different mediations, so that what I'm writing about is never about one actual mediation that actually happened that way, I've made sure that the bits I'm stitching together nevertheless *belong* together. The underlying truth, the reason why I'm telling you about it, the point I'm trying to illustrate......the thing is......it's true. It happened. All of it. It's all true.

CHAPTER ONE

My greatest mediation teacher

Zen holds that everyone we meet is our teacher. I've seen that thought attributed to the Buddha, mostly on posters that superimpose the words on a picture of a very old Tibetan person looking wise, though I've also read learned articles that say that there's no evidence that the Buddha actually said it. Whatever. As always in Zen, the point is not whether some guy who may or may not have existed did or didn't say it two thousand five hundred years ago, but rather whether the remark rings true to you. It's certainly rung true to me in my career as a mediator and so before we get into Zen and the Art of Mediation, before I even start telling you about the Four Noble Truths which lie at the very heart of Buddhism, I'm going to introduce you to the greatest mediation teacher I ever came across. Step forward and take a bow, Humphrey Forbes-Smythe QC.

That's not his real name. You probably guessed that, not least from what I said in the Introduction to this book about preserving confidentiality. Plus, if I used his real name, he might bring a libel action against me. And whilst I'm confident that I would fight it off, since what follows is, as I promised, true in its essence, it would be a little sad if a book on mediation was to spawn litigation. So we'll just call him Humphrey Forbes-Smythe. I haven't been able to find a mediator named Forbes-Smythe anywhere. So that name should be safe enough. I also tried to find a first name that no mediator anywhere has, but gave up: five minutes on the web was enough for me to conclude that the world is a big place, there's lots of mediators in it, and no matter what name one thinks of, there's a mediator, somewhere, who goes by that name. So, let's just say that if you know a mediator who is actually called Humphrey, or Forbes-Smythe come to that, then it wasn't them. OK? Anyhow, the mediator we shall call Humphrey Forbes-Smythe QC was my greatest mediation teacher because he was the mediator who couldn't mediate his way out of a paper bag. And his example will be a source of enlightenment and instruction to us throughout this book.

It must be over fifteen years ago, now, since I met Humphrey. Back then, I'd just qualified as a mediator, but I was still working in my former day job as a litigation lawyer whilst I tried to figure out how to build my practice as a mediator. My client on this occasion was a lady in her mid sixties. We'll call her Mary. Mary was being sued by a large bank, who were claiming from her the repayment of funds that they had lent to her late husband's business. He had been in the business of making those very beautiful, very traditional, welted leather shoes that feel really stiff when you first put them on, but which you know must be good for you because they cost four times the price of an ordinary shoe. The bank's case was simple: we lent money and we'd like it back, please. Before they loaned the money they had taken guarantees from Mary's (now) late husband, and also from Mary personally. The business had gone under, Mary's late husband wasn't going to be paying anything to anyone any more and the only asset around was the (quite substantial) family home that Mary and her husband had shared. The bank wanted it sold, so that the debt, or at least part of it, could be paid. They were polite. They were regretful. They didn't take any pleasure in the fact that Mary would be out on the street. But, business was business, they had loaned the money, Mary had guaranteed the loan, they were out of pocket, they owed a duty to their shareholders to recover the funds, Mary's home was the only available asset etc etc.

Mary's defence was that she may have signed the guarantees, but that she hadn't understood what she was signing. She had loved and trusted her husband, of course she had, and she'd signed because he told her to sign. She had no idea that she was putting her home on the line. And that's a defence that would have had prospects of succeeding. But, and it was a big but, she'd had legal advice from a solicitor before signing. The bank had insisted on it. And it's a lot harder to argue that one didn't know what one was signing when an independent solicitor has explained it in words of one syllable. There again, there were doubts over how independent the solicitor had been, he'd also acted for Mary's husband, and for the bank on other matters......in short, we had an argument, but no more than an argument.

In many ways, it was an ideal case for mediation. There's no villain here. The bank were out of pocket, and just wanted back some of what they'd loaned. Mary hadn't run off with the money herself. Her husband hadn't intended his businesses to go under without repaying. It was all just unfortunate. Moreover, and the bank didn't know this, Mary had neither the funds nor the will to take the case to trial. Her home, worth over £800,000, was far too big for her. She was willing to see it sold, but wanted to preserve maybe £250,000 to enable her to buy a smaller place more suited to her needs. Anything on top of that, she was willing to see go to the bank. And whilst the bank didn't know that, we guessed that they weren't really desperate for the publicity that would come with making a lady in her late sixties homeless. A deal ought to have been within reach. So when the bank issued proceedings, I put in a defence for Mary, so as to preserve her negotiating position, but we also suggested mediation. The bank agreed. They would mediate. But, the mediator had to be from one of the most expensive mediator panels in the country.

The bank's response didn't come as a surprise. I've noticed that banks and large corporations often feel more comfortable if they are paying top dollar for what is presumably a top quality service. And back then mediation was much less commonplace in this country than it now is, there were probably one or two slightly dubious mediators around, and it was no great surprise that the bank wanted a top man (or woman) at a top price as a way of guaranteeing quality. It may also have been their way of seeing whether we were committed to the mediation process. I don't know. But anyway, they named three individuals from an expensive panel, and invited us to choose one.

We went along with the suggestion. All three were eye wateringly expensive. But you'll remember that Mary wasn't in a position to take this claim to trial. She *had* to settle. And in the context of the whole claim, a few thousand pounds extra on the mediator's fee really didn't matter one way or the other. If paying a bit more for an expensive mediator was the bank's price for agreeing to mediation, it was a price that Mary was prepared to pay. So she agreed to the bank's proposal, and asked me to choose one of the three. And I chose Humphrey Forbes-Smythe QC. Yes. He was my choice. It was all my fault. Mea culpa, mea maxima culpa, as Buddhists don't say.

Humphrey had a glittering CV. He had been educated at a renowned public school, one where the termly fees are about equivalent to the GDP of a small to medium sized developing country, one where wisteria grows on the walls of ancient courtyards. He'd then read Law at a renowned university, one where wisteria grows on the walls of ancient courtyards, and where he'd won the Smoked Mackerel Prize in the Inter-Collegiate Mooting[1] competition. From there, he'd progressed to the Middle Temple, one of the Inns of Court in London, where, yes, wisteria grows on the walls of ancient courtyards, and where he'd won the Smoked Haddock Prize in the Mooting competition. After being called to the bar[2] he'd joined a prestigious set of barristers' chambers and built a successful career as a leading advocate. He'd been elevated to the lofty rank of QC about as quickly as it's possible to achieve such glory. Over and above all that, Humphrey Forbes-Smythe QC was the only one of the three suggested mediators whose CV showed that he had specialised in banking litigation. But what really sold Humphrey to me was a quote on his CV, apparently from a solicitor he'd mediated, which read "I have seen over a thousand mediators, and you are undoubtedly the best mediator in the universe". That sealed it, I'm afraid. The best mediator in the universe! It was hard to see how anyone else could improve on that. And whilst there was obviously a degree of hyperbole in the statement, this was the assessment of some battle hardened lawyer who had (apparently) seen a thousand mediators perform. And Humphrey was the best of the lot! The best in the universe. Humphrey was the man for us. And I'll admit, at the back of my mind was the thought that as a fledgling mediator myself, I couldn't but learn from a mediation with the best mediator in the universe. So, we

---

1 Mock advocacy

2 When barristers qualify they are called to the bar – the rest of us just walk straight up to it and order without waiting to qualify.

selected Humphrey Forbes-Smythe QC to be our mediator, and on the day of the mediation I travelled to London with Mary on the early train hoping and expecting that Humphrey would do the job for Mary, and rather looking forward to seeing the great man mediate.

The mediation was at the office of the bank's solicitors in the City of London. These were the kind of expensive offices that have gold framed paintings of Victorian lawyers on the wall, and where one sinks so far into the deep pile carpet that one nearly gets stuck in it and has to be dug out. The mediation was due to start at 10.00am, but I had made a point of getting there by 9.00am. I wanted Mary to feel unrushed, to have time to relax, and maybe to have a few words with the mediator before the formal start time, just to cover any questions she might have, and to help settle her nerves. The only problem was, the mediator wasn't there. Not at 9.00am. Not at 9.30am. Not even at 10.00am, when we were due to start. At about quarter past ten, I left our room and went looking for him. It turned out that he'd arrived only a few minutes earlier, and was ensconced with the bank's lawyers already, which was slightly disconcerting. I knocked on the door to introduce myself. Humphrey Forbes-Smythe QC was tall, thin, and wearing a very prominently pin striped double breasted dark grey suit, the kind that, if the films are to be believed, was de rigueur for gangsters in 1920s Chicago. His hair was parted at the side and rather short, almost aggressively so. He wore round gold rimmed dark glasses. You may recall that a few years ago, when international relations across the world were (briefly) improving, Hollywood ran out of nations to demonise and went through a phase of casting English actors in the role of the master villain in action films. They were always immaculately dressed, they always spoke in the most polished tones, and they were always bent on evil and destruction right up to the last scene when the all-American hero would defeat them with a right hook and a pithy quip. I don't know if it was the dark glasses, or the combination of those with the dark pin striped suit and the haircut, but something about Humphrey momentarily brought one of those villains to mind, a thought I quickly dismissed.

"Yes, put it over there" Humphrey said, glancing at me briefly before turning back to the bank's solicitor. As I had nothing to put over there, I was a bit thrown and just stood there for a moment, before introducing myself as the Defendant's solicitor. "Of course you are!" exclaimed Humphrey, "delighted to meet you". He seemed to be searching for my name, which he appeared not to have heard. "Delighted to meet you….old chap" he concluded, shaking my hand and beaming at me. "Now, I've only just arrived, and I'm just having a little chat with the Claimant, so why don't you run along back to your room and I'll come and join you very shortly" he said. I couldn't quite put my finger on why, but it didn't feel like the best of starts. His manner was polished and urbane, it's true, but something about it lacked warmth, and finding him ensconced with the other party before he'd even greeted us was a little disconcerting. And then, being told to "run along" back to my room wasn't great. But the privacy of each party's rooms is important in mediation, and it's not really the done thing to go and just knock into the other party's room uninvited, so perhaps I shouldn't have done that. Fair enough, I told myself, and I duly ran along back to our room where I passed on the good news that Humphrey was in the building.

About ten minutes later, nearly at 10.30am he joined us. "So sorry I'm a tad late" he said, in a tone of voice that suggested that he wasn't. "London traffic!", he went on, "Gets worse and worse, doesn't it? And then, finding somewhere to park! Parking spaces these days are so small, don't you find?" We didn't find, actually, and as we were from Norfolk we didn't feel greatly responsible for the London traffic either, but Humphrey seemed to need an apology, so we apologised anyway. He appeared mollified. "Not your fault I'm sure" he said generously, and then introduced himself: "I'm Humphrey", he said, before adding "Humphrey Forbes-Smythe QC" just in case we might have muddled him with some other Humphrey who wasn't in the mediation anyway. "And you must be Molly. Delighted to meet you, old thing". "Mary", I corrected, but Humphrey ignored me. "Right, well, we should crack on, don't you think? Don't want to be late this evening, do we? Ready for the plenary, Molly?" A plenary session is one that all the parties attend together, usually at the start of the mediation. It's probably a word that's more commonly used in the USA; in the UK, we tend to refer just to "joint sessions". At any rate, Mary hadn't heard the term. "What's a plenary?" she asked. "What's a plenary?" Humphrey repeated, wide eyed, "Dearie me". He then looked at me and asked with a smile "Has someone not explained the process to their client?" His tone was amiable enough, but nevertheless the kind of tone a nursery school teacher might use when reprimanding a child that's just returned from the toilet having forgotten to do up their trousers properly. I had of course told Mary that the mediation would probably start with a joint session, I just hadn't used the word "plenary". But before I could really follow this train of thought much further, I noticed the papers that Humphrey had brought with him and placed on the table in our room. Before the mediation both sides had, as is usual, sent Humphrey short "Position Papers", outlining our positions in summary form. These he had in loose leaf form, slightly crumpled, but I guess that showed that he'd read them. But we had also sent a folder containing the paperwork that I and the bank's solicitor had agreed Humphrey needed to see: the Claim and Defence from the court file, witness statements from Mary and from the relevant bank official, and the loan documents, together with some of the most relevant correspondence between the solicitors. What had caught my eye was that the file containing these papers, which I had prepared, was still *sealed* in the plastic wrapping in which we had sent it the previous week. Humphrey hadn't opened it. I probably shouldn't have stared at it so obviously. At any rate, Humphrey noticed my eyes fixed on it, and appeared to guess my train of thought. "If you're wondering whether I've read the paperwork you so kindly sent, old chap, I don't need to" he announced proudly, "I can settle this case without all that". Mary started to cry. Humphrey looked at her kindly. "I know", he said, "amazing, isn't it, Molly?" And with that he gathered his papers, read and unread, and led us towards the joint, or plenary, session.

The purpose of a joint session is supposed to be to give each party the chance to put their case directly to the other side, perhaps less in the expectation that anyone will change anyone else's mind than in the hope that each party will at least feel that they have got their arguments off their chest. I'll have some more to say about joint sessions in chapter four. Quite a lot more. Anyhow, in this case, Humphrey spoke first, and at some length. He told us about his experience in banking litigation, about the many cases he had fought and won (he never lost, it seemed), cases where he had been instructed on behalf of "altogether bigger banks" than the Claimant, and he told us about the cases he'd mediated (all of which, it seemed, had settled – or rather, as Humphrey phrased it, all of which *he* had settled). And he assured us that although our case was altogether smaller and less significant than those cases, he, Humphrey Forbes-Smythe QC, was today going to settle our case.

Well, that was nice. Eventually, Humphrey invited the bank's solicitor to speak. Which was fair enough. It's usual to invite the Claimant to speak first. The bank's solicitor was polite, but firm. He thanked us for attending the mediation. He told us that the bank was attending in good faith, and was hopeful that we would reach an acceptable settlement. All good, standard stuff. But, he said, any settlement would have to take account of the strength of the bank's position. Again, standard stuff, and we were expecting it (I've yet to come across a lawyer who opens the negotiation by suggesting that the settlement would no doubt reflect the fact that his clients really didn't have a leg to stand on). And he wanted to say a few words about the strength of the bank's position. That, too, we were expecting. What we weren't expecting was that he didn't get very far. Humphrey interrupted him. He began "Yes, thank you so much, old chap. I think what Mr Corporate Counsel is trying to say is.....", before expounding what he considered the bank's case to be. I wasn't quite sure what to make of this. On the one hand, I couldn't help but notice that the bank's solicitor seemed discomfited, and for all the world looked as if he hadn't realised that his case was that which Humphrey was espousing. Which felt like it might be good for us. On the other hand, I didn't recognise the case which Humphrey was setting out either and, as Mary's solicitor, it was really my job to know the case against us. It was almost as if Humphrey was dealing with a totally different case. When he finished, he then turned to me and invited me to reply for Molly. I began with the usual pleasantries. We thanked the bank for attending mediation. We too had come in good faith hoping for an acceptable settlement. You can guess the rest. We too felt that the settlement would have to reflect the strength of our case, and I proposed to set out a couple of key points. Except that I didn't get even as far as the bank's solicitor had done, because Humphrey cut me short. "And thank you too, Mr Dragon. Most helpful. If I may say so, I think what Mr Dragon means to say is…..". At the time, I had no idea why he called me Mr Dragon. It was only on the train home that evening that Mary pointed out that I was wearing a blue silk tie with a dragon motif that Karen had brought home for me when she attended a conference in China some years ago. At the time, it just confused me, though not so much as Humphrey's exposition of "Molly's" case, which followed, and about half of which I didn't recognise at all. But Humphrey wasn't to be deterred, and having set out what he considered to be "Molly's" Defence, he sent both parties to their respective rooms "to have a little ponder about what I've said", after which he said that he'd join us for a little chat. The bank's solicitor added that lunch would be served in our rooms.

With the late start, and Humphrey's rather lengthy exposition of our cases (or more accurately, his exposition of somebody else's cases, because what he had set out certainly wasn't our case) it was indeed lunch time and before long lunch was served: the kind of business lunch that was so expensive that it came with a little menu, so that we knew what good things we were eating. Mary and I were both somewhat shocked by the morning's events, and weren't hungry, but I felt that I wouldn't be helping her greatly if I confided that I really didn't feel remotely comfortable with what was going on. She needed to feel that everything was under control, I thought, so I tried to appear as confident as I could, and we made small talk whilst we waited for Humphrey to appear. And waited. And waited. Our small talk dried up. About two hours later he appeared. I don't know where he had been. Perhaps the London traffic was to blame. He sat down with a sigh that suggested weariness. His bonhomie appeared to be wearing a little thin. "Alright then Molly", he said, "I need you to give me your very best shot, old thing". Mary looked blank. It transpired that what Humphrey wanted was a settlement proposal. Our best shot at settling the case. I was surprised. I'd expected discussion of the case with both Mary and myself, consideration of the strengths and weaknesses of our position before turning to what might be settlement parameters, that kind of thing. But, by now it was early afternoon, heading into mid afternoon. Time was running on, and perhaps cutting to the chase was the best strategy. So we opened up to Humphrey. We told him that Mary had no assets other than her home, which we hoped might fetch £800,000, and that she was prepared to sell that if she could keep maybe £250,000 back to buy a modest new home for herself. That was all we had. Our best shot. Our only shot. Humphrey shook his head sadly. "Dear oh dear. We're going to have do better than that, aren't we Molly?" he said. I interjected that Mary actually couldn't do better than that. "Yes, thank you Mr Dragon" Humphrey responded, curtly I thought, before explaining that the bank's debt was well over a million pounds. Which, of course, we knew. After legal costs and the costs of selling her home, Mary's proposal wouldn't leave the bank with much over a third of their debt paid. And if he, Humphrey Forbes-Smythe QC were acting for the bank and were asked to advise on a settlement proposal in this case that allowed the Defendant to keep £250,000, he would give it short shrift. And he was sure that the bank's legal team would do the same. He knew how these people thought, and we'd simply have to do better, wouldn't we? Mary started to cry. Humphrey kindly suggested that he'd give Molly some time and space so that she could dry her tears and come up with something better. And with that he was gone.

By now, we were really starting to despair. Mary didn't have anything else to give, unless it was to concede that she should lose the roof over her head entirely. And whilst we knew that our case was a long way from being bulletproof, if the alternative was having nowhere to live at all, well, we were agreed that at that point Mary had little option but to fight.

Humphrey came back a good bit later. It was probably five o'clock. He sat down opposite Mary, crossed his legs, fixed his eyes on her, and said that he had a really important question for her. This turned out to be: "Do you want to settle this case, Molly?" Mary nodded. Yes, she did. Humphrey smiled. "Well then", he said, "We're going to have to do better, aren't we? Now, do you have a more realistic proposal for me, Molly?" I told him that we had no better proposal, and that we could have no better proposal. Mary had to keep some kind of roof over her head. Humphrey gave a resigned sigh. "If you'll forgive me saying so, old chap", he said, "it sounds as if you don't want to settle at all", before adding that he would convene another plenary session, at which he was sorry but he'd have to give us "both barrels". This was rather a scary prospect, actually, since it felt as if our mediator had been giving us both barrels pretty much all day. But, Humphrey wasn't asking whether we'd come to another plenary session, he was telling us. It was that, or call a halt to the mediation. And we needed to settle. So we agreed.

It was about six o'clock when we convened for our second plenary session. The bank's solicitor had a face like thunder. Humphrey seemed pretty cross by now, too. "It seems as if I'm the only person here thinking about settlement", he began. Then he urged Molly and Mr Dragon to consider the case the bank would be putting to the court. If he, Humphrey Forbes-Smythe QC were addressing the court on the bank's behalf he would put it in these terms. First, the bank had loaned the money. The health of our economies, and with it all of our homes and our pension funds and our prosperity, and probably civilisation as we know it, depend on the availability of credit. And here the bank was, providing credit. Doing what banks do to keep the wheels of commerce turning. He made it sound as if their motive was pure charity, which didn't quite square with the interest rates they were charging. But Humphrey was beyond such trifling considerations. Where had the money gone, he wanted to know? To Molly's husband's businesses, yes, but what was the point of those businesses? To fund the lifestyle of Molly's husband….*and Molly*. Yes, the money had gone to Molly. She had received the benefit of the money. And here she was, trying to evade liability to repay. Supposedly on the grounds that she hadn't understood what she was signing. But that wouldn't wash. Molly was an averagely intelligent lady. With a basic command of the English language. She had an education, no doubt. She understood perfectly what she had signed. And she had the benefit of legal advice before she signed. If there was something she hadn't understood, she had only to ask. But, no, she had signed, because she had wanted the money, and she had understood perfectly well what was going on. And now, finally, the time had come for her to pick up the bill for the lifestyle she had enjoyed.

Humphrey positively glowed with pride at his own eloquence. I was glowing too, but not in a good way. I told Humphrey that I recognised neither the facts nor the legal position as he had portrayed them as an accurate representation of my client's case. "Not pretty, is it?" Humphrey purred, before turning his back on me and turning instead to face the bank's solicitor. "But now, Mr Corporate Counsel, I want you to hear what I would say if I were representing Molly, because that isn't pretty either". And off he went. This case was about one thing. Whether this lady (he waved a hand in the general direction of Mary) got to live out her remaining days in her home. It wasn't much to ask for. And why was she standing before the court in peril of losing that basic human entitlement? One reason only. One word. Trust. She had trusted her husband. She had trusted her solicitor. She had trusted her Bank Manager. This was no hardened businesswoman. She wasn't particularly bright. Humphrey could assure the court of that. She had no head for figures. No understanding of business. And who should have protected her from the business deals that she didn't understand, from the figures that were above her head? Her Bank Manager, of course. He knew her. And if he didn't, he should have done! He knew – or should have known – that she had no understanding of the potential consequences of signing that guarantee. Did he not owe her a duty of care? Of course he did. And had he not failed her? Had he not abused her trust? Of course he had. And why? One reason only. One word. Profit. There stood the bank, unwilling to accept its responsibility for its own failure in this matter, motivated only by profit. The unacceptable face of capitalism.

Humphrey had finished. At least, I think he had finished. At any rate he paused for a moment, to contemplate his own oratory. The bank's solicitor was as furious as I had been. He said pretty much what I had said: that he recognised neither the facts nor the law as Humphrey had portrayed them as having any bearing on this case. "There you have it, Mr Corporate Counsel, Mr Dragon", Humphrey observed, "nobody likes it when they hear the case that's going to be presented against them by a skilled advocate". "But I've done you a favour", he continued, "because this is your chance to settle this case without having to listen to that speech again. Wouldn't that be a consummation devoutly to be wished?

So may I ever so respectfully suggest that we all reflect on that, and then I expect there might be some movement from what I'm sorry to say have been rather stubborn positions, haven't they?"

I can't now recall whether I or the bank's solicitor spoke first. But we both said the same thing. We had set out our client's positions already, and we had nothing to add.

I've told you in the Introduction that I've made changes to all the stories I've recounted in this book, in order to ensure that the identities of all involved are protected. That applies to this chapter too: every potentially identifying detail has been changed. But, reader, the account that follows of what Humphrey said and did next is as near to the truth, the whole truth, and nothing but the truth as my memory permits.

Humphrey slumped momentarily in his chair, and sighed deeply. It was if the air had gone out of a balloon. "Such a shame" he said, in a tone of voice that suggested that he really couldn't have cared less. He hauled himself back up on his elbows. His tone was cold and clipped now. "I've been signalling for some time that I need to eat", he said. He put a particular emphasis on the word "eat", sounding the final consonant, which made it sound aggressive. And then – and I promise you, he actually did this – he opened his mouth wide and pointed at it, in case we were in any doubt as to which orifice he used to consume his food. "And since no one has been taking any notice of my signals, and since it's clear that no one here apart from me has the slightest intention of settling, we're done". And with that, he got up and walked out of the room. The bundle containing the mediation case papers that I had prepared remained unopened and unread on the table. And a case that could have settled, no, that really *should* have settled, that actually *had* to settle, didn't settle.

What became of Mary? That evening, she cried all the way back to Norfolk. We set about defending the case. Just how Mary was going to fund the legal costs was unclear, but if the only alternative was losing everything she had, we had no alternative but to fight.

A few months later the court fixed a directions hearing. That's essentially a hearing where a judge and the solicitors discuss the mechanics of getting the case to trial. What do we need to do, and by when? How long to exchange our documentary evidence? How long to exchange witness statements? How many days does the court need to set aside for the trial? That kind of thing. I attended, as did the bank's solicitor. After the hearing, I asked the bank's solicitor if I could buy him a coffee: he agreed. And over that coffee I asked him what he had thought of the mediator. Not much, he said. But then, he said, if the Defendant had come to the mediation unwilling to contemplate any kind of concession, what could the mediator do? I had to ask him to repeat himself. *He* thought *we* had come to the mediation unwilling to contemplate any kind of concession? He did indeed. It transpired that while Humphrey had been telling poor Mary that her offer to sell her home was totally unrealistic, he had been telling the bank that their wish to see Mary sell her home was, in effect, the unacceptable face of capitalism.

After that, things moved pretty quickly. I spoke to Mary, and we made an offer to sell her house on terms that she kept £300,000 back. The bank came back agreeing to the principle that Mary could keep something from the sale proceeds as the price of a settlement, but suggesting a figure of £200,000. Well, there was a figure in the middle, which began with a 2, then had a 5 in it, and then had lots of noughts, which was kind of the figure we'd first thought of, and we settled at that. Mary's house, which was far too big for her, was put on the market, and sold for something over £800,000 in a rising market. Mary kept a roof over her head, and the bank's shareholders saw some recovery of the monies that the bank had loaned, quite possibly as much as if they'd pursued the case all the way to trial and won but incurred hugely increased legal costs along the way, and a case that should have settled, that actually *had* to settle, did settle.

Mary bought a modest bungalow on the North Norfolk coast. There are beaches in North Norfolk where the sand and the sea and the sky go on forever, and where the whole world is made anew with each new tide. You should visit. And if you do, and if you see a white haired lady, who by now would be getting on in years, walking her Labrador on the beach, it might be Mary. There again, it might not. Labradors are pretty much compulsory on Norfolk beaches.

And what became of Humphrey Forbes-Smythe QC? Well, I never saw him again. About six months after Mary's mediation, I had cause to look again at the mediation provider that had supplied Humphrey, and I noticed that he was no longer on their panel. I wasn't able to find out much: everyone seemed rather tight lipped on the subject of Humphrey Forbes-Smythe QC. It seemed that he had decided to pursue his illustrious career as an advocate in preference to his no doubt equally illustrious mediation career. And yet, the odd thing is, not only did I never see or hear about him again, I never came across a single case report that mentioned him as instructed for either side. And when I searched for him on the internet as I wrote this book, even the all-seeing eye of Google couldn't come up with any information about Humphrey Forbes-Smythe QC. It's as if the intervening years have wiped him out of history. Nothing beside remains.

But wherever you are, Humphrey, and whatever you're doing now, I bring my hands together in the Buddhist gesture of gratitude, and I bow in your general direction. Everyone we meet is our teacher. And I learnt more from Humphrey in one day than I learned in my whole time at Mediator School. I learned how *not* to mediate.

Trainee mediators have to observe more experienced mediators as part of their mediation training and a few weeks ago in London a trainee mediator who had observed me mediate said to me that I always seemed to know what to do next, even when the situation seemed deeply unpromising. Yes, I know. It was almost certainly said to flatter me. Sadly, I don't in fact have any special ability that enables me to know what to do next in every mediation. But I do have a secret, and I will share it with you now, reader. Which of course means it won't be a secret any more. But, hey, you've paid for this book, so you're entitled to something in return.

When the going gets tough, when the parties are entrenched, when there's no movement, when the mediation is just going nowhere, and when I know that if the next thing I try doesn't work then one side or the other is going to walk out, I do this. I find the kitchen, and I make myself a cup of tea. Tea is always good. And whilst I wait for the kettle to boil I ask myself: "What would Humphrey Forbes-Smythe QC do now?"

And then I do the opposite.

CHAPTER TWO

The First Noble Truth

Buddhist legend has it that the Buddha meditated for six years before realising his "First Noble Truth". The First Noble Truth is usually translated as "All life is (or involves) suffering" or sometimes "All life is unsatisfactory", though I was told by a Buddhist monk, who I assume knew what he was talking about, that the word the Buddha used, *dukkha*, actually translates not so much as "suffering" but as "stuck", in the sense of a wheel that won't turn. So perhaps "Life doesn't run smoothly" or even "People get stuck" would be a better translation. At any rate, it's probably the First Noble Truth that leads many to believe that Buddhism is a miserable religion, particularly those who never got past it to Noble Truths Two to Four (which are about the cause of, and the cure for, suffering). If the Buddha had consulted a marketing consultant he would have been told that to make a new religion marketable his First Noble Truth ought to catch the consumer's interest right from the start with the promise of something good; eternal life, 10% off the wages of sin, unlimited chocolate, that sort of thing. But if they had marketing consultants 2,500 years ago, the Buddha wasn't interested, he just told it how he saw it, and after six years' meditation he concluded that life, on the whole, just doesn't always run smoothly.

I don't know if the Buddha really meditated for six years before coming to this conclusion. It sounds pretty implausible to me. For a start, he would have had to get up in between times to eat, to sleep and to answer the call of nature. Perhaps the point is simply that he meditated for a long time, and the figure of six years isn't to be taken too literally. But I do know this. It wouldn't have taken the Buddha six years to conclude that life is unsatisfactory if he had supported Norwich City Football Club. A Saturday afternoon would have been enough. Karen and I have season tickets to Norwich City's home games, and we've lost count of the ways in which the boys in yellow and green can snatch defeat from the jaws of victory. Sometimes, they manage to snatch defeat not so much from the jaws as from the oesophagus of victory. Life just isn't entirely satisfactory.

The Buddha advised the good folk of Kalama not to believe anything just because he said it, but to test everything he said against their own experience. I'm guessing, however, that the proposition that "Life is unsatisfactory" or "Life doesn't always run smoothly" isn't one that requires a lot of testing. Like a lot of the Buddha's "truths" it's actually pretty obvious. You may think that the truth is, actually, obvious more often than not. At any rate, I'm not advancing a particularly radical proposition if I join with the Buddha in stating that a sense that life is unsatisfactory now and then is, like death and taxes, a universal human experience. No doubt death and taxes have something to do with that.

This universal human experience – the Buddha's First Noble Truth – is also the starting point for the mediator mediating any case. The people who are in dispute aren't satisfied with their life. It's not running smoothly. For a start, they don't generally want to be in dispute. Chances are they find the whole existence of the dispute thoroughly unsatisfactory. In a host of different ways, perhaps, but the common thread is that they don't want to be in dispute. Some are outraged that anyone could make a claim or complaint against them. Others will be equally outraged that anyone could seek to defend or rebut their self evidently justified claim or complaint. Some will regret the damage the dispute does to their family, or perhaps to their relations with neighbours, or to their business. Others will be angry at the time and effort the dispute demands, or perhaps at the money it swallows up in legal costs. All happy folk are alike, but each disputant is unhappy after their own fashion, as Tolstoy almost wrote. But what they all share is that they are unhappy.

As mediators, we must start from the recognition that we are dealing with people who are unhappy. Not necessarily about everything in their lives, but about being in dispute. Which means that the first question for us as mediators is: what do people who are unhappy or dissatisfied want?

Put your hand up if you read that question and thought: "They want the cause of their unhappiness or dissatisfaction removed". Actually, before you put your hand up, just check that you are in a situation where doing so won't be socially inappropriate, or otherwise cause you personal embarrassment or even lead to legal complications. Whether or not you put your hand up, if you thought that, then, well done, because that may indeed be what they want. Perhaps, ultimately, removing the cause of their dissatisfaction is what everyone wants. But it's not always quite that simple.

If you had met me in a Manchester street after a mediation one Friday a couple of months ago then when I asked you the way to the railway station, you might have guessed that I was feeling dissatisfied. I needed to know the location of the station, I didn't know it, the last train that would get me home was about to leave in ten minutes, and the seven people I had already asked had all said "Railway station? No idea, mate". In this instance, all I wanted was the location of the railway station. I didn't need anyone to feel my pain, just telling me where the station was and how to get there would have done nicely, thank you very much.

On the other hand, a few months ago I mediated an inheritance dispute in London. On that occasion, when I met the long term partner of the deceased, she told me "I've lost the love of my life and I just don't know what to do any more". Now, she knew perfectly well that I couldn't remove the cause of her unhappiness and restore her partner to her. She wasn't expecting that. She wasn't even wanting me to tell her what to do now. She wanted something more than that, actually. She wanted me to recognise her pain, and thereby to affirm her pain, and in so doing, affirm her. And if I'd responded "Well, that's a shame, but what you should do now is settle this case quickly so that we can all go home, and you could pass me the coffee whilst you're at it", that wouldn't have been appropriate.

Sometimes we just want information. Like the location of the railway station. And we'll use that information to deal with the cause of our dissatisfaction. Sometimes there's another simple solution to a problem.

Mostly, however, we want something *more* than just a solution. We want affirmation. Having our feelings affirmed is a basic human need, and I'd say it's often as fundamental, or even *more* fundamental, than providing a specific solution to a particular problem.

The Buddha and the man with 83 problems

There's a story about a businessman who came to see the Buddha to ask for his help....

A businessman had heard that the Buddha was a great teacher, and could solve many problems, and he apparently felt that he had many problems. His problems were weighing him down and, frankly, making his life a misery, and no one seemed able to help him with them, or to offer any advice at all. So, he travelled a great distance in order to ask the Buddha for help.

The Buddha greeted him kindly, and asked him just what his problem was. The man needed little encouragement.

"I'm a timber merchant," he began, "I buy raw timber from the growers, cut and season it, and sell it on for all kinds of uses; homes, furniture, tools, ships, you name it, anything, really. And I like that; it's a great business. It's what my father did before me, and his father before him. But, well, the first thing is that the king, who is one of my biggest customers, needs to cut his cloth in order to fund his endless wars, and he's insisting that I sell my timber for less than I did last year. And I can't afford to lose his custom, besides which, he's the king, and it doesn't do to fall out with the king. But I couldn't source the timber for 10% less than the last year at the best of times. And these aren't the best of times! Quite the opposite! There's been too much rain, and that's affected the quantity and quality of the timber. A lot of it has gone bad and that in turn has sent the price of what's left sky high, even though in other years it would be classed as second-rate product. And that's another thing. The king is insisting on higher quality across the board, he claims my rivals have promised to deliver higher quality, at lesser cost. And how am I supposed to produce higher quality for less when it's costing me more to purchase inferior stock, I'd like to know?"

The man seems to have gone on. And on. One problem seemed to lead to another. His employees wanted to be paid more, and didn't seem to appreciate that he could only pay from profits, and it didn't look like he was going to make any profits any time soon. All they thought about were themselves. And he had a wife. And she was a good wife; he even loved her. But sometimes she nagged him too much. And sometimes, well, he wondered if he could do better. And he had kids. And they were good kids. He enjoyed them a lot. But sometimes….

The Buddha listened intently to the businessman's story until finally the businessman finished. Then the Buddha said; "Ah. I see. You have 83 problems".

The businessman was impressed: "Is it that many? Well, I knew it was a lot, but 83, is it really that many? No wonder I've been feeling awful. They keep me awake at night, you know. You must be a very wise teacher. 83, is it that many? Yes, I suppose it must be. Well, then, how many of my 83 problems can you help me with?"

"None of them", replied the Buddha.

"I'm sorry", said the businessman, "for a moment there I thought you said that you couldn't help with any of my 83 problems".

"That's right", said the Buddha.

The businessman was startled. He said, "I thought you were a great teacher. I thought you could help me."

"Well, it's like this," said the Buddha. "We all have 83 problems, each one of us, and there's nothing anyone can do about it. If I could somehow manage to solve one of your 83 problems, another would immediately pop up to replace it. It's just a fact, a law of nature. You'll always have 83 problems, we all will. There's nothing you nor I nor anyone else can do about it."

The businessman was furious. "Do you have any idea how far I've travelled to ask for your help? Can you begin to contemplate what it's cost me, in time and money to come here? And you can't solve one tiny little problem out of my 83 problems! Not one! What good are you? What good is your teaching? What exactly can you help with?"

"Well," said the Buddha, "I only help with the eighty-fourth problem."

"The eighty-fourth problem?" said the man. "What's the eighty-fourth problem?"

"The eighty fourth problem", said the Buddha," is not wanting to have the 83 problems".

Whether the businessman punched the Buddha in the face is not recorded. But there's much wisdom for the mediator in the story of the Buddha and the man with the 83 problems, and we'll touch on it again in a later chapter. For now, the point is simply the Buddha's comment that if he could somehow manage to solve one of the businessman's 83 problems, another would immediately pop up to replace it. The point isn't the number 83 itself. That's almost certainly not meant to be taken literally. If you have too much time on your hands, or otherwise need to get a life, and you stopped to count, you would have noticed that there weren't actually 83 problems in the story. It's a figure of speech, and the point is that solving a particular problem doesn't make "everything all right", at least not for long. Even though at the time when you have a problem you may think that dealing with that problem is all you need to be completely happy, solving that problem won't prevent another one popping up at some point, and probably sooner rather than later. Nobody, ever, lives (completely) happily ever after. Which is why fairy stories end "And they all lived happily ever after" and history books don't.

Recognition and affirmation

By the time we've got beyond fairy stories we've learned from experience that we're never going to solve all of our problems forever. Life, as the Buddha noted in his First Noble Truth, won't always run smoothly. And as a species, homo sapiens have developed a mechanism for coping with this state of affairs. We may always have problems, indeed *we will always* have problems, but we feel better about our problems, and are better able to become "unstuck" and move on from them, if we can share those problems with someone else, and that other person recognises and affirms the feelings we have about those problems.

Why does having our feelings recognised and affirmed make us feel better? I don't know. That's not my field. But I know from my own observations that it does. And if, as the Buddha suggested to the folk at Kalama, you don't want to take someone else's word for it, then good for you: you don't have to. Try the following thought experiment.

Janet comes into the room to find John hot and bothered over a new piece of electrical equipment that he has bought. He greets her with

> "This is so frustrating! I've wasted half an hour trying to set this thing up! The instructions are completely incomprehensible, and whoever translated them clearly couldn't speak a word of English. And the diagrams are worse, and make no sense at all, and as far as I can work out, contradict what little sense I can make of the instructions! Look, this should switch it on, here, and I try it and try it and nothing happens! It's maddening!"

We've all been there. Put yourself in John's shoes, and see how two different responses from Janet affect your feelings. Here's the first:

> "Have you tried plugging it in?"

And here's the second:

> "Yes, isn't it maddening! I had the same problem with something else just the other day. You'd think they could just produce a few

lines of simple, plain English. And, those diagrams – worse than useless! So annoying! I tell you what, though, just a thought, have you tried plugging it in?"

The first response may be the answer to the problem. In his eagerness, John forgot to plug in the device. John may be grateful to have that pointed out. But the first response is still likely to leave John feeling frustrated. Perhaps even more frustrated than he was before Janet gave him the answer. The second is likely to leave John feeling a whole lot better, as well as grateful for the answer.

Why? The answer to John's problem is word for word the same in each example: "Have you tried plugging it in?" But in the first example, Janet has not recognised and affirmed John's feelings. Indeed, by ignoring his feelings, and just giving him the (simple) solution, she may have hurt his feelings. John may feel an implication that he was being stupid and shouldn't have got so upset: far from having his feelings recognised and affirmed, John may perceive Janet to have belittled them. Though Janet didn't express it in these terms, and may not have intended it in this way, John may, in effect, hear: "D'oh! Plug it in, Dumbo!" We've all seen this kind of exchange escalate into a full-blown row: John feels belittled and responds less than graciously, and Janet, in turn, feels annoyed because John isn't grateful to her for solving his problem. Whereas in the second example, John's feelings have been recognised, and affirmed. As a result, John might even laugh at his own failure to plug in the device.

When life is unsatisfactory, we may well want the cause of our dissatisfaction removed, but that's not all we want, or even, necessarily, the first thing we want. Like John in our thought experiment, we all have an inbuilt need to have our feelings recognised, and affirmed, *before* (and regardless of whether) the problem can be solved. And the skilled mediator or dispute resolver will look to demonstrate recognition and affirmation of the feelings of the people involved right at the start.

You may of course be thinking: why? Why, as a mediator should I be concerned with recognising and affirming other people's feelings? You may feel that your concern is to get a deal, to end the dispute, not to feel other people's pain. If you're thinking that, it's a good point. It's a good point if you're not thinking it, actually. The answer is that the art of mediation is the art of generating *movement*. To help people to become unstuck, to move from fixed, quite possibly diametrically opposed, and very probably intransigent positions towards a deal. And if I've learned one thing in over fifteen years mediating, it's this: *people don't move until they feel that their position and the way they feel has been recognised and affirmed*. When you think about it, why would they? If I had a few pounds for every time I've heard something like "No one understands where I'm coming from, so it's no wonder that the other side's offer is unrealistic" then, well, I wouldn't have needed to write this book for a start. If Janet and John are in dispute, and, as far as John is concerned, Janet doesn't "get" John's position or how he feels then, from John's perspective, Janet's proposals are, by definition, unrealistic because they self evidently don't take into account what is most real to John; his perspective, his feelings! People rarely if ever settle a dispute unless they feel that their position and how they feel about it has been recognised. Not necessarily agreed with, but recognised and affirmed. And whilst it would be right to say that offering someone affirmation won't immediately generate a move in their position, it is a necessary precondition if they are to become unstuck.

I would like to think that most professional dispute resolvers would probably agree the proposition that for a party to a dispute to be willing to move, they have to feel that their position has been recognised, but I suspect that as a result many focus on demonstrating an understanding of the intellectual arguments being deployed. I wouldn't disagree that an element of that may be necessary. But our need to have our *feelings* recognised and affirmed is more fundamental than our need to have our intellectual arguments acknowledged. The arguments, in the final analysis, are just the tools with which we disagree. Once upon a time, in the distant past, we resolved disputes by sharpening our weapons and perhaps hiring champions to do battle on our behalf. Nowadays, the use of force to resolve disputes is (generally) considered uncivilised. So instead of deploying arms, we sharpen our arguments (or pay someone else to sharpen them for us) and then hurl them at each other. But the dispute isn't fundamentally about the arguments deployed, any more than trial by combat was about the weapons used. We have all seen instances where someone's arguments start to unravel. I've seen it in more mediations than I can count. What happens? Do people drop their flawed arguments and abandon their position? How many times, in over a thousand mediations, would you guess that I've head someone say "Do you know what, listening to what the other side say, I've come to the view that my position is intellectually flawed and morally wrong, and I've decided to concede this argument"? Well, here's a clue: you could count the number of times I've heard that, or even anything remotely like that, on the fingers of no hands. If their arguments are undermined, people don't abandon their positions; they just think of new arguments. Or, they refuse to acknowledge that their arguments are coming apart at the seams. Or they get cross (and more intransigent!): "I haven't come to this mediation to debate the rights and wrongs!" And that's not surprising. The dispute wasn't about the arguments in the first place. The dispute was about each side's feeling that they were entitled to something more than the other side were willing to give. The arguments were just the means to reach the desired end. And demonstrating that those arguments may be flawed doesn't touch someone's feeling that they are entitled to whatever they were arguing for. In fact, it makes them feel crosser and more angry, and therefore *less* likely to move, because, by demonstrating that the arguments being advanced are flawed, the other party is actually demonstrating precisely that they *don't* recognise and accept the feelings behind those arguments.

In a mediation I sometimes hear "Your argument is wrong, so you shouldn't feel that way". Sorry, but that's the wrong way round, folks. Nobody feels a particular way *because* they have an intellectually sustainable argument. Try telling your spouse, life partner or significant other that when you first met them you didn't feel any emotions towards them but instead made a cold intellectual assessment of their suitability to be the love of your life, taking into account their intellect, emotional make up, earning capacity, and physical attractiveness and, having concluded that they were suitable when judged against these criteria, you decided to tell them that you loved them. Actually, don't try that: I don't want to be responsible for the ending of a beautiful relationship. But you get the point. In a dispute, as in a relationship, the argument or analysis follows the emotions, and is simply an attempt to justify the position to which a disputant *feels* entitled. So, since people won't generally move their negotiating stance until their position has been recognised and affirmed, the skilled mediator or dispute resolver must seek to demonstrate not just an understanding of the arguments being employed, but, more importantly, to convey recognition and affirmation of the *feelings* of the people involved.

What's the distinction between recognition and affirmation? Recognition – that is, simply to perceive, and to identify, someone's emotional state – doesn't help much. To say:

"I can see that you are upset about being in this position"

recognises another's emotional state, but that recognition remains distant and carries no hint of affirmation. Recognition on its own won't get the mediator far: more is needed. Sympathy goes a bit further: it involves recognising someone's emotional state, and to feel sorry for them:

"I can see that you are upset about being in this position, and I'm sorry to see that."

That's going to do more, in terms of helping people to move, because it involves at least a small degree of emotional involvement (feeling sorry for the person). But again, sympathy can remain quite distant, and stops short of what is needed, which is affirming the feelings in question. To affirm another's emotional state involves demonstrating, at its lowest, that one recognises another's feelings, that one understands them, *and that those feelings are ok*. To say:

"I can see that you are upset about being in this position, and that's only natural"

takes a (small) step from recognition to affirmation. And the more the mediator or dispute resolver is able to convey a degree of empathy, the stronger the affirmation will be, and consequently the greater will be the subsequent ability to get the disputant to move their position. Empathy requires not just recognition of someone else's emotional state, but an ability to share it (at least to some degree, at least for a moment, at least to some extent). To feel empathy for someone is to "put oneself in their shoes":

> "I can see that you are upset about being in this position, and that's only natural, in your position I'd be feeling exactly the same."

And the more empathy the mediator feels and is able to convey, the better.

Empathy

At this point, I can hear alarm bells going off in the brains of any of my fellow mediators who have read to this point. Sorry, folks, and thanks for sticking with me this far! The problem is that mediators are often taught that as a mediator you should not show, or even feel, empathy but should remain "professional" and detached. The idea is that allowing your own emotions to be engaged would compromise your detachment and professionalism. Which, according to the traditional view, would be bad, since as a mediator, if you become emotionally involved, you would no longer be independent. I get that. And, just for the record, as a mediator I stand or fall by my independence. A biased mediator is less use than a chocolate teapot.

But, here's the thing. An empathetic emotional response to someone else's pain is both *natural* and, in the context of dispute resolution, *helpful*. And it needn't mean any loss of independence for the mediator or dispute resolver.

Last year, I gave Karen a bird box for Christmas. With a hidden camera in it, that sends pictures of what is happening inside the box back to a computer. It's a nifty little box, and it didn't take us much more than 45 hours to get it working. As a result, last Spring we were able to watch blue tits building their nest inside the box, and laying eggs from which, miraculously, cute little baby blue tits appeared. Well, to be completely honest with you, when they appeared they weren't actually very cute, but they soon became both cute and fluffy. When they fledged and flew off we were almost as proud and emotional as if we were their parents. We spent happy afternoons looking at young blue tits feeding in the garden and trying to identify which were "our" blue tits. But, some didn't make it. They died. In the nest, or when they tried to leave it without having worked out that this flying business requires flapping their little wings. And how did we feel when we picked up the lifeless body of one of the blue tits? We felt sad. Not inconsolably so, no. We didn't cry ourselves to sleep for nights afterwards. They're only blue tits. But, nevertheless, our natural emotional reaction was to feel (a bit) sad.

Now, I don't mean to trivialise the upset or anger of the people I'm mediating by comparing their woes to the death of baby blue tits. In a sense, the relative triviality of the death of a baby blue tit[1] is precisely the point: it shows that our *natural* response to pain or loss in another sentient being is to feel at least a degree of compassion, even where the loss to us personally is small or non-existent. Now, you may say that a dead blue tit, or, say, an injured kitten, or a crying child, prompts a particular emotional response from us because they are small, fluffy and cute, and we're hardwired to respond emotionally to small, fluffy cute things. And I guess that's so. But we're also hardwired to respond with empathy to the pain or loss of other human beings even where they're not small, fluffy or cute. Moreover, and this is the really exciting bit for the mediator, this natural response really is helpful to the process of dispute resolution. If people feel that we understand and affirm their feelings, and in particular feel empathy for their dissatisfaction or hurt, they are more likely to move their position when we suggest to them that they might have to. This reaction is absolutely key to successful mediation but once again you don't have to take my word for it, so if you're up for it, we'll try another thought experiment.

The thought experiment begins with a scene I witnessed one evening last winter when returning from mediating a commercial dispute in

---

1 Yes, I know. It's not trivial to the blue tit.

London. It had been a cold week, with several trains cancelled or delayed due to frozen points, frozen signals and, for all I know, frozen drivers. My mediation had run late, and I had only just made the last train home from London, and I was feeling quite pleased with myself about that when the conductor announced that we'd all have to get off again. The train had been cancelled due to a problem with the brakes, and the only hope of getting home at all was that the railway company were going to try to "source a coach". Clearly, this wasn't great news. For starters, when someone says that they are going to "source" something, what they usually mean is "we haven't got one and we don't know where to find one". Added to which, once the coach was sourced, we all knew that a coach from London to darkest Norfolk would take at least an hour longer than the train would have done. So, it wasn't great news, and for one chap who'd clearly had a particularly trying week, it was just one problem too many. He was furious. He had paid a fortune for his season ticket! And the service just got worse and worse! Every day this week there'd been some delay on the trains! And now this! Well, he'd had enough, and he wasn't going to get off this train! They'd just have to find someone to sort the problem out and get it moving.

Here's the thought experiment: imagine, if you will, that it fell to you to (literally) move our frustrated friend. Imagine, also, that you work for the railway company and therefore that telling their esteemed season ticket holder to just get over himself and grow up is not an option. Would you:

1. Remain professional, polite, detached, and appeal to his reason?

   or

2. Show empathy for his feelings?

Ok? Feel free to write your answer on a postcard, if you like, but there's no need to send it to me because, as it happened, I got to see both approaches. First, the conductor from the railway company tried option 1: professional, very polite, but detached, and appealing to our friend's reason:

"I can't allow you to stay on the train, Sir. You'll just have to get off. The train is going nowhere, Sir. The brakes have failed. You wouldn't want us to run the service with defective brakes would you? Come on now, Sir, I'll have to ask you to get off this train and get on the coach."

How do you think that worked? Not well, I'm afraid. Our friend just got crosser and crosser. He knew the brakes had failed, damn it! And whose problem was that? The railway company's problem! He paid good money to them to provide a working train, and if the train wasn't working, that was jolly well their problem, not his, and they'd best get it working! And he wasn't going anywhere until they did.

After a while, the nice lady from the buffet car came along with a cup of tea and tried option 2: showing empathy:

"I know, Sir. It's awful. You're quite right. It's been a disaster of a week and what a way to end it! The truth is, the new rolling stock can't come fast enough, can it? And until it does, you're asked to put up with this. Not good enough at all, is it? I'm so sorry, Sir. If there were anything else I could do, I'd do it, but I'm afraid the only thing I can do is to get you on the coach which has just arrived and will get you home as soon as possible."

That worked. Our friend got on the coach, still complaining, and entertained the rest of us with his interesting views until he fell asleep somewhere north east of London.

If you chose option 2, you may now give yourself a congratulatory pat on the back[2]. Although I'm guessing that the fact that option 2 – showing empathy – worked better than the approach that remained emotionally detached and relied on the perfectly reasonable point that you wouldn't actually want the train to run with defective brakes would you, Sir, won't have come as a great surprise. We all intuitively know that on a personal level if someone is upset, showing a degree of empathy will help to resolve the situation. But when it comes to

---

2 For Health & Safety reasons, if you are holding this book in one hand, please pat yourself on the back with the other hand

training professional mediators, the approach of too many mediation schools is to teach would-be mediators that they must (in the name of "impartiality" and "professionalism") supress any empathy they might naturally feel, even though that empathy would be helpful to the dispute resolution process. What's more, those same mediation schools then to go on to teach those same would-be mediators a range of techniques designed to compensate for the fact that the mediator is not feeling empathy so as to give the parties to the dispute the impression that the mediator nevertheless understands and affirms their position It would be enough to make me tear my hair out, if I had any left. Please don't misunderstand me: there's nothing wrong with the techniques they teach. It's just that teaching the techniques whilst forbidding the natural empathy that would empower those same techniques is, well, it's the mediation equivalent of building a car, ripping the engine out, and then telling the driver to get pedalling. The greater the empathy the mediator is able to convey, the greater the trust in the mediator that will be generated, and the greater the trust in the mediator, the greater the movement the mediator may be able to coax from the parties to the dispute.

There's a Zen story about a monk walking along the bank of a deep river. He wants to cross, and he sees another monk walking along the opposite bank. So he calls out: "Brother, how do I get across to the other side?" The second monk replies: "Brother, you are already on the other side". Which, you may think, wasn't the most helpful of answers[3]. But you'll have got the point. We all see things from our own perspective. And we can't help others to find their way – whether that way lies across a river, or whether it's from an entrenched position to a mediated settlement – until we can find a way to share their perspective. If you want to help someone to move, if you want to help them in any way at all, *you have to go to where they are*. To start from where they're

---

3 The story is often told to illustrate a different point: that we're so often searching for something that we think is elsewhere when, actually, if we were just to stop searching everywhere but where we are, we'd see that the thing we're looking for is right in front of our noses. In that sense, the second monk is offering the first monk a helpful lesson. But for our purposes, and taken literally, the fact remains that as directions go, it's just not a helpful reply!

starting. Not necessarily physically, but in terms of sharing their perspective, intellectually and emotionally, to see and to feel the world at least to some degree as they do. To stand, as it were, on their side of the river. As my colleague and fellow mediator at mediation 1st[4], Susan Blake, says: "What works for me is to get alongside a party".

But what about impartiality, I hear the Mediation Police cry. What about professionalism? Isn't there a risk that if you allow yourself to feel empathy, you may end up feeling more empathy for one side than the other, and therefore favouring them? Well, here's the thing: feeling empathy for someone doesn't mean that you agree with them, or prefer them to anyone else, or even that you can't feel similar empathy for their opponent in the dispute. Karen and I feel sad for the baby blue tits that don't make it. That doesn't mean we prefer them to the ones that do make it, or that we have made a value judgement that their parents were bad parents. We just feel sad. It's a natural reaction. I'm guessing that the nice lady from the buffet car on the late night London to Norwich train didn't agree with the angry customer's plan to stage a midnight sit-in on the train until the fairies appeared to mend the brakes. But, she didn't have to *agree* with him to feel a natural empathy for a very unhappy human being facing a delayed trip home, and it was that empathy that gave her words the power to move him. Nor would the second monk in the story have had to forget which side of the river he was on in order to see the world from the first monk's perspective and to understand which side the first monk considered to be the "other" side. And as a mediator, I think it's natural to feel a degree of empathy when faced with people who are dissatisfied and upset. That feeling doesn't imply a value judgement about the strength of one side's case as opposed to that of their opponent, or as to what the terms of the settlement should be. In fact, it's perfectly possible to feel empathy for both sides without judging between them.

Just a couple of days ago I mediated a dispute between two siblings in the fair city of Cambridge. The brother claimed that the sizeable contri-

---

4   Mediation 1st is my little mediation business. We call it that (a) to distinguish it from mediation 2nd (D'oh!) and (b) because the websites for the other names were already taken.

bution he'd paid to the purchase of his sister's home meant he owned a share of that home and could now force a sale and pocket a tidy profit. The sister said the money was simply a family loan, that it didn't give him a share of the property, and that she didn't want to sell what was not only her home but also the home she'd bought together with her deceased partner and the "last thing she had left of him", and moreover that her home was the "only safe place" for her young children all of whom had quite enough to do coming to terms with the death of their father as it was. She spent a lot of the early part of the mediation in tears. Did I feel empathy for her? Of course I did. She'd already lost her partner, and the father of her children, she now faced losing her home, and it looked rather like she'd lost her only sibling as well. One would have to be made of stone not to feel empathy for her plight. Did I show that empathy in private sessions with her? Of course I did. I don't know what definition of the mediator's role requires the mediator to behave as if they have as much feeling as an under-boiled cauliflower in circumstances where any human being would feel empathy. But did that empathy blind me to the fact that the brother had a point of view too? To the fact that he had actually borrowed money on his own home to make the purchase of a home for his sister possible, that he'd been paying interest on that borrowing for years so that she could have a home, that he was now forced by circumstances beyond his control to demand the return of what he'd put into his sister's house if he wasn't to lose his own house, and that he didn't feel the least bit good about that but why should he lose his home so that she could stay in hers? No, I wasn't blinded to any of that. I felt empathy for his position too. Nor did the empathy I felt for the sister mean that I couldn't see that ultimately she and her lawyer accepted that, even on her case, her brother's money was a loan, which in law had to be paid back (loans tend to work that way, I'm afraid) and that given her lack of other funds the only way to repay her brother was going to be out of the sale proceeds of her home anyway. What the empathy I felt – and showed – for the sister did mean was that she was actually open to having a conversation with me about the sad reality that there really was no scenario in which the house didn't have to be sold and that perhaps she had to come to terms with that. Whereas once her brother felt that I empathised with his position and didn't see him as the bad guy making his sister homeless, he was willing to have a conversation with me about why he needed the money, just how much money he needed, and exactly when he needed it by. And, yes, brother and sister found a solution and the case settled.

Now, a word of warning here. Caveat mediator. Don't let the example I've just given lead you to conflate empathy with putting an arm round someone's shoulder and offering them a box of tissues whilst they have a good cry. That may be appropriate in mediation. Sometimes. Perhaps in some of the inheritance disputes I've mediated. A metaphorical arm round the shoulder was certainly appropriate in the example of the brother and sister that I've just told you about. And, yes, every mediator should carry some tissues. Preferably nice, clean, presentable ones. But if I'd offered the angry businessman I mediated in Leeds the other week (who greeted me with "Time is money, I just want this sorted") a box of tissues and suggested that before we sort out his dispute he might need a good cry, he would have been apoplectic. He was pretty apoplectic as it was, actually. In his case, empathy meant something rather more obviously dynamic than tissues and sympathy. Empathising with someone means to put yourself in their shoes, to see the world from their perspective. For my friend in Leeds empathy meant a brisk and business like approach to cracking the tiresome dispute that he was stuck in.

A word the Buddha used a lot in this context was "compassion". Ok, that's probably not true. To be completely accurate, the Buddha wouldn't have used the word "compassion", because he didn't speak English, he spoke Pali, and he'd have used the Pali word "karuṇā" which is usually translated into English as "compassion". But although our word "compassion" is a close approximation to the Buddhist concept of "karuṇā", there is a subtle but significant distinction between our concept of "compassion" and the Buddhist concept. In fact, I've come across Buddhist writers who use "karuṇā" in preference to our own word "compassion", even when they're writing English, so as to signal that subtle distinction. That doesn't really work for me, I'm afraid: "karuṇā" just sounds too much like a cold beer, so, if you'll bear with me, I'll explain the distinction between the way we use the word "compassion" and the Buddhist concept, because that distinction is critical to the mediator's mind set and to what I mean when I say that empathy, which is very closely related to compassion, at least in the Buddhist sense, can empower your mediation techniques.

An online search for synonyms for "compassion" comes up with "sympathy, pity, fellow feeling, solicitude, tenderness, gentleness, and charity". Now, don't get me wrong. These are all great qualities. But taken together they're probably a bit, well, a bit passive for the Buddhist interpretation of karuṇā, and also for the mediator's role. They're firmly in arm-round-the-shoulder-would-you-like-a-tissue territory. They wouldn't have gone down at all well with my friend in Leeds. The Buddhist notion of karuṇā is or at least can be altogether more dynamic. It's a kind of active compassion. A muscular compassion if you like.

Let me introduce you to a figure from the Tibetan Buddhist tradition. She's the Bodhisattva Tara. Who, or perhaps what, is the Bodhisattva Tara when she's at home, you may ask? And what's a bodhisattva, come to that? Now, that's a big question. Too big for this book, I'm afraid. If enough people buy this book, and my publisher commissions a sequel entitled "Zen and the Art of Loads More Zen"[5] we'll do a whole chapter on bodhisattvas. I promise. For the present, suffice to say that a bodhisattva represents an ideal of helping others, and in Tibetan Buddhism Tara is the Bodhisattva of Compassion. Now, before the Zen Police jump on me, I should clarify that in Japan, where Zen originated, if you say that Tara is the Bodhisattva of Compassion you may get some blank looks. In the Zen tradition, the Bodhisattva of Compassion is called Kanzeon, and (like Tara) is female. Whereas in the Tibetan Buddhist tradition, the Bodhisattva of Compassion has a male aspect, who goes by the catchy name of Avalokiteshvara, and a female aspect, which is Tara. In some Tibetan stories, Tara came from Avalokiteshvara's tears. Which, you may think, sounds pretty implausible. But, hey, it's a metaphor. A beautiful way to say that compassion grows out of empathy. That's all. And it's a particular aspect of the traditional Tibetan Tara figurines that I'm going to write about here, hence the

---

5 It works for me.

appearance of a figure from the Tibetan Buddhist tradition in a book about Zen and the Art of Mediation.

Anyhow, you don't need to think of a bodhisattva as some kind of divine (or non-divine, come to that) being. Instead, you might like to think of the Bodhisattva Tara as simply an embodiment, or perhaps *the* embodiment, of the quality of compassion. I saw Tara figurines all over Nepal when I visited that beautiful country, and indeed you can buy brass figures of Tara in almost any online Buddhist store[6]. Like many bodhisattva figures, she's usually depicted as seated cross-legged in meditation. Except that she's not. Look closely, and you can usually tell if a bodhisattva figurine is Tara because one of her legs is raised. She's getting up. Rising from her meditation. Going somewhere. She may be the Bodhisattva of Compassion, "She Who Hears the Cries of the World" but she doesn't just sit there having a good cry about the cries of the world. She's off to do something about them. The answer to the question "Who, or what, is the Bodhisattva Tara when she's at home?" is that, mostly, she's not at home. She's out there in the world, doing her Bodhisattva of Compassion thing. That's compassion in Buddhism. When it needs to be, it's active, it's dynamic.

And like Buddhist compassion, a mediator's empathy can be dynamic, brisk and business like, or it can be solicitous, sensitive and understanding. Empathy is the magic dust that enables the mediator to be what they need to be to establish a connection with just about anyone. And as I hope my Cambridge mediation between brother and sister shows, and as I've found on countless mediations, in every case I've mediated, actually, one can feel empathy for both sides. Empathy doesn't arise out of an intellectual evaluation of either side's case. It doesn't imply agreement with anyone's position. It has nothing whatsoever to do with the strength or otherwise of anyone's argument. I've never felt empathy for a legal proposition. Empathy doesn't arise in

---

6 Just to confuse matters, there are "White Tara" and "Green Tara" figures, for reasons we won't go into now. If as a result of this chapter your heart's desire were to be a Tara figurine like the one I'm about to describe, you'll need to be in the "Green Tara" section of your friendly local online Buddhist store.

response to legal propositions. Legal propositions just aren't that interesting.

There were many reasons why Humphrey Forbes-Smythe QC couldn't mediate his way out of a paper bag. It would be quicker to list the things he did right than the things he got wrong. But if I had to give one reason, and one only, as to why Humphrey made such a dog's breakfast of mediating Mary's case, it would be this: he felt no empathy. He didn't care about Mary. Everything about him – the way he looked, the fact that he arrived late, the fact that he hadn't read the papers, the fact that he couldn't remember Mary's name, the way he talked to, or rather at, Mary, the way he used words that she didn't understand, the way he interrupted the lawyers or called them names, the way he disappeared for large chunks of the day without explaining where he was or what he was doing – everything he did said "I DON'T CARE" just as clearly as if he'd had the words tattooed in capital letters on his forehead. He didn't care about the bank, either. He was incapable of feeling empathy, of putting himself in someone else's shoes, because he hadn't noticed that there were any shoes in the room other than his own immaculately polished ones.

The Buddha's First Noble Truth is that people are dissatisfied with and stuck in their lives. In the context of a mediation what people are dissatisfied with and stuck in is their dispute. The mediator is likely to feel empathy not because they agree with either side's intellectual or legal position, but simply because the people in dispute are dissatisfied, miserable, and stuck, and it's natural for most of us to feel empathy for people who are dissatisfied, miserable, and stuck, probably because we've all been in that place at some point in our lives. Those of us who support Norwich City more often than most. And the mediator's first job is to offer those stuck individuals the sense of affirmation that they need in order to be able to move on and find a solution to their dispute. Empathising with them helps to do that, and will empower your mediation techniques. It's as simple as that.

CHAPTER THREE

The Second Noble Truth

Noble Truths, it seems, are like buses. You wait six years for one, and then four come along at once. The Buddha supposedly meditated for six long years without so much as a single solitary truth, noble or otherwise, showing up. Then, on the day of the first full moon in December he went into a forest near what is now the town of Bodhgaya in northern India and sat down to meditate and, a week or so later, on the eighth day after the full moon, four Noble Truths came along one after the other[1].

The Second Noble Truth is often translated as being "The Truth of the Origin of Suffering" or "The Truth of Craving". The reason for our *dukkh*a, our suffering or dissatisfaction, for the way our lives are stuck, is that in our ignorance we desire or crave what we do not have. Craving. It's not a word we use much nowadays. I don't know if the Buddha really spoke like an extra from a film version of the King James' Bible who has accidentally strayed onto the set of a Buddhist movie, or whether the folk who first translated the Buddhist texts just thought that their translations would have more gravitas if they made the Buddha sound that way. My money is on the latter. Anyway, the truth of craving is simply that, dissatisfied as we are with the world, we desire it to be other than it is.

Pretty obvious, hey? We're unhappy because the world isn't as we desire it to be. Or is it that the world isn't as we desire it to be, because we're unhappy? There's room to debate which is cause and which is effect here. Indeed, there are Buddhist scholars who have had a good time doing so. At least, I hope they were having a good time, because I'm all in favour of good times, and I can't see that they were achieving much else. For my part, I'm not sure that there has to be one cause and one effect. If they're both true then perhaps they're just both true, interde-

---

[1] At any rate, the eighth day after the first full moon in December is the date in the Zen tradition. Other dates are available in other Buddhist traditions.

pendent, or, if you prefer, facets of the same truth. We're unhappy because we desire the world to be other than it is, and we desire the world to be other than it is because we're not happy with the world as it is.

What's more, Zen teachers emphasise that we don't just desire the world to be other than it is, we tell ourselves stories about why it *should*, really *should*, be other than it is. For example, last weekend Norwich City lost. Again. And I can tell you now, it just wasn't *fair*. The other side's goal was offside. The ref was biased. The linesman was biased. The half-time tea lady was probably biased. We were unlucky. The ball just wouldn't run for us. We *shouldn't* have lost. We had more possession than them. More corners than them. More shots than them. We were the *better* team. Basically, we thrashed them 0-1. And anyway, the other side spent far more on their team than we did, and so it wasn't a *fair* contest in the first place. If there were any *justice*, any *fairness* in the world, we'd have won. We *should*, we *should*, we *should* have won.

And so on. We all have a soundtrack inside our heads that tells us how things should be. Everyone's will be different, but they'll all contain lots of "*shoulds*" and lots of "*shouldn'ts*", lots of "*fairs*" and lots of "*unfairs*", a lot of "*I*" and a lot of "*me*", and a lot of "*want*" and a lot of "*should have*". Now, don't get me wrong. Neither the Buddha nor I are saying that it's necessarily *bad* to think this way and that we *shouldn't* have such thoughts. That would just be another story about the world, another "*shouldn't*". The point is a different one. These stories about how the world *should* be don't make us happier. On the contrary, we beat ourselves up with them. Not only does convincing myself that Norwich City should have won at the weekend not improve the score line, it probably makes me feel worse. I'm now nursing a sense of injustice to go with my disappointment. And these stories that we tell ourselves are stories because in the real world as opposed to in my head there's no "should" or "shouldn't" about Norwich City winning. There's a chain of cause and effect about why they lost, no doubt, but no "should" or "shouldn't". The universe doesn't care about Norwich City[2]. And "fair" or "unfair" doesn't come into it. The value judge-

---

2 Self evidently.

ments that we tell ourselves the universe ought to conform to have no objective existence in the world.

You don't agree? Fair enough. (Oops! You see how pervasive that word "fair" is?). But, yes, fair enough, if you don't agree, go and find "fairness", and bring it to me. Go on. No, not the word "fairness". I know where that is, in the dictionary, after "faint" and before "fairy"[3]. I don't want an example of "fairness" or someone's opinion that something is "fair". Not even something that you consider fair, dear reader, notwithstanding the fact that your purchase of this book marks you out as an individual of high discernment. I mean the thing itself. *Fairness*. Bring me *fairness*.

No? Can't find it? That's because it's a subjective value judgement, a concept whose existence is located in our minds, in the stories we tell ourselves about how the world is and how it should be.

Language and cinders

I thought about writing that concepts like *fairness* exist *only* in our minds, but perhaps that's not quite true. They also exist in language. Now, whilst language may be the product of our minds, you could argue that language exists outside our minds in speech, books and other written records. And language is an extraordinary thing. The basis of our communication, the foundation of our culture, and supposedly one of the things that distinguishes human beings from other animals. Though I'm not sure about the last point. My wife Karen speaks fluent Cat, and knows exactly what our cats' different meows mean. Or perhaps the cats speak Karen, which may explain why she lets them and their muddy paws into bed every night. Either way, there seems to be a shared language of sorts there. But even if other animals have some basic communication, human language remains an amazing thing, and because it's so powerful it's easy to think that if something exists in language, in the sense that we have a word for it – *good, bad, fair, unfair,*

---

3 They don't have any objective existence in the real world either. Sorry.

and all the rest – then the word must correspond to something in the real world. But just because the words exist that enable me to say:

"I saw an invisible pink unicorn last night"

doesn't mean that I did, or that anyone ever has, or ever could. In fact, the miracle of language here enables us to create a notion in words that is doubly impossible in the real world:

i. a *sighting* of an *invisible* unicorn
ii. which despite its *invisibility*, has a *colour*.

The First World War poet and thinker, T E Hulme, saw the world as "cinders" – fragmented, chaotic, and blowing in the wind – and language as a kind of grid that floats freely above the cinders. In Hulme's vision language contains its own internal structure and points of reference, but ultimately remains disconnected from the cinders. You can see what he means. The meaning of words is ultimately subjective, not fixed. They mean what they mean because we all decide that they refer to a particular thing in the world, but if we decided that they were to refer to something else in the world, then they would; the meaning of words can shift. One of my favourite poems is the medieval English poem, Sir Gawain and the Green Knight. In the poem, Sir Gawain, who is one of the knights of King Arthur's round table, is fond of referring to "King Arthur and his gay knights". In the late fourteenth century that meant that King Arthur's knights were mirthful, jovial, and habitually in good spirits. The word "gay" continued to mean broadly that for the next six centuries. If you like, Hulme's language grid remained sitting more or less over the same cinders. But in the second half of the twentieth century, the word "gay" acquired a new primary meaning: it denotes someone who is romantically attracted to others of their own gender. The old medieval meaning of "gay" is still there, in the background, and some of the aspects of the word's earlier meaning probably explain why it came to bear its new meaning, but the fact is that the primary meaning of the word is now radically changed. If we were to refer today to "King Arthur and his gay knights", we'd be saying something about Camelot that wasn't in the mind of the writer of Sir Gawain and the Green Knight (so far as we know). The winds of time have blown the cinders about under the grid so that the word now corresponds to a different meaning.

Hulme's vision of a grid floating over but disconnected from the cinders of reality applies equally well to a legal system. A legal system is an organisational structure that we create, sure, but its value judgements – *lawful* and *unlawful*, *legal* and *illegal*[4], *fair* and *unfair*, *rightful* and *wrongful*, *equitable* and *inequitable*, and so on – aren't eternally fixed and can be shifted. To stick with the example of sexuality, sexual intercourse between two males was illegal until 1967 (in England and Wales), 1981 (in Scotland) and 1982 (in Northern Ireland). Intercourse between two females, oddly, was always legal, supposedly because when asked to sign the legislation making female homosexuality illegal, Queen Victoria refused to believe that such a thing could exist[5]. The fact that sexual intercourse could be legal or illegal depending on your gender and/or that of your partner, the date upon which you had sex, and your precise location within the United Kingdom when you had it, ought to demonstrate that legal judgements do not represent eternal verities.

We tend to look upon the insight that the meaning of words and concepts (even moral or legal concepts) is not fixed but shifts with time and place, and that what we believe and teach to be *right* and *wrong* or *lawful* and *unlawful* may not be eternal verities but the products of a given time and culture as a rather cutting edge modern idea. Indeed, T E Hulme was considered to be at the leading edge of the "modernist" movement along with such luminaries as T S Eliot and Ezra Pound. Well, perhaps there's really nothing new or modern in the world, because the Buddha got there two and a half millennia before the modernists:

---

4 Do you know the difference between "unlawful" and "illegal"? No? "Unlawful" means something is against the law, whereas "illegal" is a sick bird of prey.

5 I have my doubts about the accuracy of this story, actually, but the myth (if that's what it is) is persistent.

> "I perceive the teachings of the world to be the illusion of magicians....I look upon the judgement of right and wrong as the serpentine dance of a dragon, and the rise and fall of beliefs as but traces left by the four seasons."

I've come to particularly like the Buddha's image of the judgement of right and wrong as "the serpentine dance of a dragon". Before I became a mediator, it resonated less for me: it was a nice image, but that was all. But in a mediation, as I go from one side's room to the other, I see how each side takes each moral or legal argument advanced by the other side and turns it inside out, and it is as if the twists and turns of the argument are coiling through each room: the serpentine dance of the Buddha's dragon.

And just as the stories we tell ourselves about how the world *should* be don't make us any happier, so all the moral and all the legal arguments don't help us find a solution in a mediation either. Quite the reverse. Each side listens only to its own arguments, each reinforcing their own mental narrative with the conviction that *justice* and *morality* is on their side, to the point where they don't even have their own permission to move towards a compromise. How could they, when their position is *right*, is *just*, is *fair*, is *legally sound*? To move would be to betray those very concepts. And so all the fine words and the moral postures and the legal arguments become the ditches and the trenches that divide the parties from each other and which keep them out of the no-man's land in between their positions where a settlement might lie.

But what about Morality?

What about trying to live well and do good? What about ultimate moral values, shining like the stars beyond our flawed human judgements? What about *Goodness*?

Ah. Yes. What indeed? Am I saying that the Law is a set of arbitrary rules and that *lawful* and *unlawful* are just the postures of the skilled mediation advocate? That *Good* and *Bad* are just the local customs of a particular place at a particular time? That the universe has no ultimate moral compass, and that as a consequence we're all free to run around doing awful, terrible things like coveting our neighbours' oxen, or going on seal-clubbing package holidays, or supporting Manchester United instead of our local team? No, I'm not saying any of that. Not at all. There is, I know, a perception in the West that Buddhism in general, and Zen in particular, denies the possibility of "goodness" and is all about accepting the world as it is without trying to change it for the better. This perception is so wide of the mark that it's hard to know where to start to correct it. But you've paid good money for this book, which means my throwing my hands up in despair and saying that I don't know where to begin won't really cut it, so I'll do my best. Plus, I think this is really important for the mediator's mindset. So, here goes.

Does the Law have a moral basis? Are there ultimate values of *Good* and *Bad*, shining like the stars beyond our subjective and unreliable judgements? Does the universe in fact have a moral core, woven into its fabric, either because a Creator made it that way or because it just evolved that way?

I don't know. It may do. Nothing – not one word – in what follows is intended to imply that it doesn't. But this I do know. If there are ultimate values shining like the stars they are, like the stars, beyond the grasp of most people, most of the time. As a species, we humans appear to have an inbuilt tendency consciously or subconsciously to align moral or legal values with what we perceive to be our own self-interest. How many times, in all those cases that I've mediated, do you imagine that I have mediated a dispute between a good party and a bad party? Between a party that was right and a party that was wrong? Between a party with a lawful position and a party with an unlawful position? You've probably guessed: not once. Every case I've ever mediated has been a dispute between a party that was moral, right and had the law on their side on the one hand and, on the other hand, an opposing party that was, well, that was moral, right and, yes, that had the law on their side. Every one of the four hundred plus inheritance disputes I've mediated was between a party that really, really didn't care about the money and was only fighting in order to give effect to the wishes of the dear deceased and another party that really, really didn't care about the money and was only fighting to…..well, you get the general picture. I'm prepared to bet that no mediator has ever mediated a dispute between right and wrong, or lawful and unlawful. We're always mediating between right and right, between lawful and lawful. Almost as soon as a mediator enters either side's room at the start of the mediation it becomes apparent that the party in question has appropriated all the moral and legal values that could possibly touch upon the case to their own position. And so has the other side. Hulme's grid of language floats freely over the cinders of the mediation, and each party simply pulls the words and the moral judgements they need into the position that suits their own self-interest. As in mediation, so in the wider world. If the human race ever manages to wipe itself off the face of our beautiful planet, and if all of our achievements are to sink back beneath the primordial mud, and if all of our civilising values are to be lost forever in the eternal night then it won't be because there are too many *bad* people in the world: it will be because there are too many *good* people, blinded by the blazing light of their own righteousness from seeing the consequences of the oh so moral conflict on which they are embarked.

Ah, you may say, but that's just fallible human beings being human, not to mention being fallible. That doesn't mean that from some higher perspective there isn't always a right and a wrong position, a good and a bad outcome, and specifically in mediation, a better and a worse way to settle the case. The Creator of the Universe, if there is one, might look in on our mediation and have a higher view. I wouldn't argue with anyone who says it is so, since I have no way of knowing if there is a Creator, or if so, whether they are looking in on our mediation, or, if they were to look in, whether they have formed a higher view, let alone what it might be. All I ask is that we don't confuse our own personal self-interest with said higher view, which I'm afraid is what people are inclined to do. My point isn't that there is or isn't a higher view, it's that our tendency to conflate the notion of a higher view with our own interest means that appealing to a higher view in a mediation (or, I suspect, in most other contexts) is about as much use as appealing to the opinion of the Invisible Pink Unicorn. She[6], by definition, is

---

6 You didn't know the Invisible Pink Unicorn was female?

invisible, and therefore if she exists at all, she is beyond our ken. And a higher moral view, is, by definition, higher, and therefore equally beyond our ken. All that our appeals to a higher moral or legal perspective tend to demonstrate is that we can't help telling ourselves (and anyone else who will listen) stories in which we are *in the right* and the world (or some subset of the people in it) is just stubbornly refusing to be as it or they *should, should, should* be. Nor did the Buddha teach that there is no such thing as a higher or better perspective, just that we're not so good at seeing it: you'll have noted that his magnificent image of the serpentine dance of a dragon referred to "*the judgement* of right and wrong", that is to say, to the human ability to determine it, not to whether there is such a thing as right and wrong.

And whilst we're at it, no, the Zen perspective isn't that because we can't reliably tell what ultimate moral values might be in a given case we may just as well not bother about how we live. It's more the reverse. The Zen experience is that through our meditation practice we can start to recognise our internal mental narrative, the one that tells us these stories about *good* and *bad* and *right* and *wrong* and which is so full of *I* and *me* and *want* and *should*, for what it is. Which is that it is just a story – a story made of illusory values woven to advance our own self-interest (and, indeed, our own perhaps illusory sense of self[7]). What's more, as we learn to recognise this story for what it is, we can maybe turn the volume of the narrative down a little, or perhaps just learn to listen to the story it tells a little less. And we may just become a little less full of "*I*", "*me*" and "*should*" and all the rest, and we might be surprised at what flowers in the space that opens up then.

So, is that the answer to getting people to move in a mediation then? Once we've affirmed their position, and built the trust that will enable us to generate movement later in the mediation, all we have to do is to still their mental soundtrack? Well, er, yes, it's a nice thought, and up to a point it's correct. If the mediation is to settle, the mediator is going to have to help the parties pay a bit less attention to the mental soundtracks that deny them the permission to settle. But simply switching off the mental soundtrack is, well, it's difficult. It's almost as

---

7 But that's another story altogether.

58 • ZEN AND THE ART OF MEDIATION

difficult as trying to stop breathing. But, as ever, you don't have to take my word for it. Let's try it. Switching off the mental soundtrack, I mean. Not stopping breathing. I'd like you to try Zen meditation. Now, I promised in the Introduction to this book that we wouldn't burn any incense, and that there would be no chanting, and there won't be. But I didn't say anything about no meditation. It won't take long. It won't be uncomfortable. Or embarrassing. I promise. And I think it's really important to try this for yourself in order to understand what's going on in a mediation.

Zazen

Zazen is Zen meditation. It's also the name of one of our cats, though her friends call her Zaza. Anyhow, you can ignore that for now. Zazen is a Japanese word: if you were paying attention earlier you'll know already that *zen* means "meditation". *Za* means "seated", so zazen is just seated meditation. I guess it's easier than bicycling meditation. And I want this to be easy. I'll run you through the basics.

Start by positioning yourself so that you can see a watch, or a clock, or can use a timer. You need to know when we're done. I don't want to be responsible for large numbers of people spending the whole day meditating because they couldn't see a clock and didn't know when they'd finished. Just think of the loss of productivity across the economy.

Then, sit comfortably. That's the main thing. No, you don't have to fold your legs into the shape of a pretzel. Nor rest the back of your hands on your knees with the thumb and forefinger making a circle, like the models you've seen looking blissed out in posters. I would confidently predict that none of them have ever sat so much as five minutes' zazen. As Zen Master Dogen said in his Rules for Meditation, which are the best guide to zazen out there, sit *comfortably*. The clue is in the word "comfortable". Folding your legs into a pretzel shape isn't comfortable, not for most westerners anyway. If we were meant to sit folded up like a pretzel we'd all come with a choice of savoury or sweet toppings. Ok, if you're young and supple and you practice yoga, and you have a certificate from three independent doctors saying that you won't damage your knees, then, fine, go ahead, sit pretzel style. But for everyone else, just sit comfortably.

Sit with your back and neck straight, ideally with your knees below the level of your hips. Why? It just makes your breathing easier and more comfortable. You may need to put a cushion or a large book on your chair to get your hips above your knees. For the litigation lawyers amongst you, I've found that The Civil Procedure Rules serve very well here, and it's good to find a use for them. Otherwise, just sit on a chair and don't worry about the height of your knees in relation to your hips. We're not going to do this for long. You'll be fine.

Rest your hands in your lap, with the palms of both hands facing upwards, then place the palm of your left hand in the palm of your right hand, with your thumbs touching. There seem to be two schools of thought as to why we do this when we sit zazen. One says that the circular shape our hands then make represents the deep underlying unity of the universe. The other says that you've got to do something with your hands, and this is as comfortable as anything else. Me, I'm in the "Gotta do something with your hands" camp.

Take a couple of deep breaths, then let your breathing become normal. Rest your attention on your breathing. On your posture. On the fact of sitting. Focus on the moment. I had promised myself that I would write a book on Zen and the Art of Mediation without using the word "mindful". I've nothing against mindfulness, you understand: on the contrary, the concept may even have originated with the Buddha (it's part of his Noble Eightfold Path, of which, more in chapter seven) but in its modern incarnation it can too often involve doing things that you've done perfectly satisfactorily all your life but now doing them as a consumer experience. You sit, or stand, or walk, or whatever, but, hey, you're doing it mindfully because you're paying to do it to whale music[8]. So, I wasn't going to use the word. But it's no good: here it comes. Sit mindfully. Then, and this is the thing, let your thoughts go.

---

8 Ok. That was probably unfair. Sorry.

Don't try not to think. If you're repeating to yourself "I must not think, I must not think, I must not think", those are thoughts, ok?

Dogen in his Rules for Meditation said something along these lines:

> *Many thoughts will crowd into your mind. Be aware that your mind is thinking, but do not follow the thoughts. Let them go. Do not try to think. Do not try not to think. Just sit, with no deliberate thought.*

When thoughts come – and they will – don't beat yourself up for having had a thought. Self harm really isn't a thing in Zen meditation. Just notice that you've been thinking, but don't follow the thought. Like Dogen said, let it go, and return your attention to sitting in the moment.

Should be easy, no? Just sit, with no deliberate thought. How hard can it be? And we're going to give this a go for all of five minutes. The Buddha allegedly sat zazen for six years, if you believe the legend, but I'm asking you to do five minutes. You can do that, surely? Not thinking for five short minutes, what could be easier? Are you ready? Back and neck straight, left hand in the palm of the right, thumbs touching, deep breaths, rest your attention in the moment…. and you're off. I'll see you on the other side.

So, how did you do? Did you manage to stop thinking for five short minutes? To still your internal mental narrative for that brief space of time? No? How about two minutes? Still no? One minute? Thirty seconds? No? Or perhaps your mind just kept on running, your mental narrative leaping unbidden from thought to thought?

Well, don't worry. I couldn't do five minutes without thinking either. Nor two minutes, nor one minute, nor thirty seconds. Not even fifteen seconds, I suspect. Actually, whilst in this chapter we've been focussing on not thinking, because our ability (or otherwise) to still the mental soundtrack in a mediation is what we're looking at here, sitting there vacantly isn't even what zazen is meant to be about. Like Old Mother Hubbard's bare cupboard, there's nothing that great about being vacant. But, I digress. The point at hand is whether the mental soundtrack can be switched off at will for any length of time, and, yes, sometimes, when I sit zazen, I do think I'm getting there. And that's exactly the problem. I *think* I'm getting there. "Ha! This is it! I'm approaching supreme enlightenment, at one with the universe. Not a thought….except for the thought of not having a thought, dammit! Shouldn't think. Should have put the cooker on, though. Perhaps I did put the cooker on? Pretty sure I put the cooker on. Bother. Thinking again. No, Zaza, don't climb on my lap, how can I not think when you're sticking your claws into me? Ouch! Perhaps I should check if I put the cooker on…..". And so on. Our mind just keeps leaping from thought to thought like a hyperactive monkey swinging from branch to branch through our mental jungle. I can't take the credit for that image, by the way: it's the Buddha's. He referred to our internal mental soundtrack as the "monkey mind", and he had some seriously interesting things to say about our monkey mind and how it is responsible for how we see the world and how we see ourselves in relation to the world. But my Editor kindly reminds me that this book is called "Zen and the Art of Mediation" not "Zen and the Art of even more Zen", so we'll pursue the point only in so far as it relates to mediation. Which is this. If we can't manage, when we're sitting calmly without distractions, to still our internal mental narrative for five minutes – in fact, if we can't manage to still it for thirty seconds – what chance is there that anything a mediator might do could possibly still the mental soundtrack of the parties to a dispute in the tense environment of a mediation, with all the mental distractions that come with a hard negotiation, for the six or more hours that the mediation may take?

That was a rhetorical question, by the way. There's no chance. But you knew that. In a mediation, with their opponent just down the corridor in another room, and about to negotiate a possible settlement of the dispute that has blighted their lives for months or years, each party's mental soundtrack will be running in overtime, spewing out "*rights*" and "*wrongs*", "*fairs*" and "*unfairs*", "*shoulds*" and "*shouldn'ts*", with all those value judgements lighting up their indignation.

So, no, the answer to how we get people to move in a mediation isn't to somehow switch off their mental soundtrack. That's not going to happen. There has to be another approach. And for that, we need another Noble Truth. But don't worry, Sir, Madam, there'll be another one along directly.

CHAPTER FOUR

The Third Noble Truth

So, can you guess the Third Noble Truth as it applies to mediation?

The First Noble Truth is that life is *dukkha*. It's not satisfactory. It just doesn't run smoothly.

The Second Noble Truth is that part of the reason we're dissatisfied is that in our ignorance we desire the world to be other than it is, and that we get attached to the stories we tell ourselves about how the world *should* be, rather than accepting it as it is.

And the Third Noble Truth is.....

that the more we can release ourselves from our attachment to those stories about how the world *should* be, and the more we can *accept the world as it is*, the more our dissatisfaction will diminish.

Did you get it? If so, you may award yourself 100 Buddha Points, and instruct your family and friends from henceforth to address you with "O Thou Buddha of Our Age". Or maybe not, if you think that might get embarrassing in public.

We can find the Third Noble Truth in mediation too. The First Noble Truth tells us that the parties are thoroughly dissatisfied with the dispute in which they're stuck, and are therefore in need of affirmation and empathy before they can contemplate moving. The Second Noble Truth says that they're each attached to their own individual mental narratives that tell them how the world *should* be, how the case *ought* to be decided, and how the dispute *should* be resolved, that whilst they're listening to that narrative, they're not likely to move their positions, but that it's not so easy to just switch that narrative off. And the Third Noble Truth tells us that if we can get them to stop listening to that narrative quite so much and to accept the world as it is then we may be able to help them move forward.

You may think that's another Noble Truth to file under "Statements of the Blindingly Obvious". Buddhism is a bit like that. It tends to be concerned with what's right in front of your nose. If you want esoteric secrets, vouched safe only to the chosen few, then I fear that Buddhism isn't for you. The Truth in Buddhism isn't so much "Out There" as "Right Here". But if the proposition that we may need to help those in dispute listen a little less to their internal mental narrative that tells them how the world *should* be and how their dispute *should* be resolved, and a little more on dealing with the world *as it actually is*, is pretty obvious, I'm afraid that at this point there's a fair few mediators, and negotiators too, who make a false turn. They decide that the answer to getting movement is to confront each party with the opposing case.

A slap in the face with a wet fish

My old Dad used to say that something unpleasant might still be "better than being slapped in the face with a wet fish". I'm not aware that anyone ever slapped him in the face with a wet fish, actually, but it doesn't sound a pleasant experience. Well, confronting the parties to a dispute with the other side's case is the slap-in-the-face-with-a-wet-fish phase of a mediation. It's often said to be a form of "Reality Testing", and the idea is that having won a party's trust, and thereby got them to drop their guard, the mediator then slaps them round the face with a wet fish. Whoops, sorry, slip of the tongue, meant to say: having won a party's trust the mediator then "reality tests" their position by confronting them with the opposing case.

The notion that this is a good idea is sort of understandable. First off, if each side's mental soundtrack is preventing them from accepting a compromise, it's not inherently a daft idea that one might present them with the opposing soundtrack. Then, most mediators, at least in the UK, are lawyers by trade. And in the UK, we pride ourselves on our adversarial system of justice. This system is founded on the notion that the best way to establish what's right in a given case is to have the two opposing sides bash bits out of each other with legal argument in front of a referee (also known as a judge) who then picks one side and declares them the winner. A little like a reality TV show, only without the TV bit (and arguably without the reality bit too). As a result, the idea that the path to ultimate truth, or at least to a sensible resolution, lies through a clash of opposing arguments is second nature to most lawyers schooled in the adversarial system. And although many legal systems don't adopt the adversarial model (preferring instead the radical notion that the best way to find justice in a given case is to have someone independent look for it – far out, no?) the idea that a confrontation between opposing perspectives is the way to progress beyond those perspectives is deeply ingrained in western philosophy. The German philosopher Johann Gottlieb Fichte proposed that new ideas come about as the result of the clash of a *thesis* with an *antithesis*, which clash results in a new notion, a *synthesis*. This is known in philosophy as the Dialectic Method and, for reasons that are unclear to me, is usually attributed to another German philosopher, Georg Wilhelm Friedrich Hegel, who never actually used the terms. But, at any rate, the Dialectic Method has a respectable philosophical pedigree, and therefore the notion that the mediator should treat each side's case as a thesis, to be confronted with the antithesis of the other side's case, in the hope that the clash yields a settlement by way of a synthesis, is a respectable proposition. I don't disagree with it because it's not intellectually sound, or because it doesn't have a decent theoretical pedigree. I disagree with it because it doesn't work.

I could just tell you that I know it doesn't work because I've seen it tried loads of times. Which I have. With uniformly unsuccessful results. But, like the Buddha at Kalama, I don't want you to have to take anything on trust.

So, let's start by having a look at the opening scene of one of the greatest plays ever written: Shakespeare's King Lear. You may be familiar with the scene. The old and irascible king, Lear, has decided that he is going to abdicate and divide his kingdom between his three daughters. He's going to do this in public, and he has invited anyone who is anyone to the ceremony. So, it's a big do, and before handing over his kingdom the king invites his daughters in turn to say how much they love him. It's a bit like the mediation of an inheritance dispute, where the parties to the dispute each profess that they loved the deceased the most, and that the only thing they're interested in is the wishes of the deceased, except that here Lear is still very much alive and very much kicking. Anyway, his two eldest daughters, Goneril and Regan, duly oblige, making flowery speeches in which they profess just how much they love their old dad. Gonerils' conclusion:

"Beyond all manner of so much, I love you"

gives you a flavour. Now, you could say that they're being a tad over the top, hypocritical even. If you know the rest of the story (spoiler alert!) you probably would say that. But actually Lear is like a party to a mediation with a mental soundtrack running in his head, in this case all about how great a king he is, how generous he is to give his kingdom to his daughters, how much they should love him etc etc, and Goneril and Regan are simply affirming his mental narrative, reflecting back the value judgements of that soundtrack. And it works. Dad is pleased and dishes out a third of his kingdom to each. Then, we get to the proposed climax of the ceremony. Lear turns to his youngest, and favourite, daughter, Cordelia, to whom he proposes to give "a third [of the kingdom] more opulent than the rest"[1]. The old man asks his favourite daughter what she can say to surpass what her sisters have said, and sits back to enjoy what he's about to hear. But Cordelia replies, simply: "Nothing".

Now, she's not saying she doesn't love her old dad. The question was: what can you, Cordelia, say that goes beyond what your sisters have said, in order to get the best piece of the kingdom ("What can you *say*, To draw a third more opulent than your sisters?"). And Cordelia's response, reasonably enough, is that since her sisters have used up all the hyperbole going, there's actually, literally, *nothing* she can say that would go further. Dad, however, is displeased. We can imagine his mental soundtrack. This was supposed to be the climax of the ceremony. Of his entire reign, probably. His favourite daughter telling the world she loves him the most. Which, no doubt, he feels he richly

---

[1] Yes, I know. If it's "more opulent" than the rest, then they're not thirds. No doubt that was part of the problem.

deserves. And here she is refusing to do that little thing for him, leaving him with egg on his face in front of some seriously important people. He's cross, but he gives Cordelia the chance to speak again. And what does Cordelia do? She decides to confront his mental soundtrack with reason. To point out that her sisters can't, and probably *shouldn't*, love him to the exclusion of everything and everyone else:

> "Why have my sisters husbands, if they say, They love you all......
>
> Sure, I shall never marry like my sisters, To love my father all".

Now, you may think Cordelia is at some level *right*. Perhaps at every level. Her sisters' declarations of love for their dad were wildly over the top. What's more, (spoiler alert again!) you may know the story, or simply guess from what I've told you, that Goneril and Regan are probably bad eggs and not to be trusted, and will turn on Dad as soon as they have the chance, and you may feel that Cordelia probably has their number. I wouldn't argue with any of that. But here's the thing. Cordelia may be right. Her point may be well made. But, what she's doing is confronting Lear's mental narrative with an opposing narrative. The thesis of Lear's question meets the antithesis of Cordelia's reply, and what happens? Does Lear say something like:

> "Ah, ok. That's a fair point. Now you put it like that, I see that there's a perfectly reasonable opposing point of view. What we need here is a synthesis of our two opposing perspectives, a compromise between your need for plain speaking and my need for a bit of public ceremony and affirmation. Tell you what, why don't we convene a mediation to see if we can agree on an appropriate form of words?"

Er, no. He just gets crosser. In fact, the more Cordelia confronts him, the crosser he gets. At first, he's willing to give her a second chance ("Mend your speech a little, Lest it mar your fortunes") but when she persists in putting her opposing point of view to him, he completely blows his top:

"Here I disclaim all my paternal care…and as a stranger to my heart and me, Hold thee thus forever".

After which, it's pretty much downhill all the way. Cordelia is disinherited and has to go into exile, the kingdom is divided between Goneril and Regan who waste little time in turning on their old dad, there's a civil war, and it ends badly for just about everyone. Oops. Gave the ending away! Sorry. My bad. But, hey, how much of a surprise is it really? It's called "The *Tragedy* of King Lear" after all. It was never likely to end in a family group hug, was it?

Of course, you might say that King Lear is just fiction. Lear doesn't respond well to being confronted with the opposing point of view, but then Lear isn't a real person. He doesn't have a mental narrative, actually, because he's just words on a page. Fair enough. That's true. There again, Shakespeare is one of the greatest writers in history not just because of his ability to make words sing in iambic pentameter, but also because of his uncanny insight into how real people actually behave in the real world. And that's the point. Lear's behaviour in that scene is just so plausible. So utterly predictable. So human. It rings true. And I've seen it in mediations. Too often. Confront the other party with the opposing case, and all that happens is that the confronted party's own mental narrative just gets more strident.

There are a fair few mediators who do this confrontation in a fairly abrupt slap-around-the-face-with-a-wet-fish way. With, I'm afraid, predictable results: the trust the mediator has built up is lost. Humphrey Forbes-Smythe's mediation style, you will recall, consisted almost entirely of slap-in-the-face-with-a-wet-fish confrontation. And frankly, rather than be mediated by Humphrey Forbes-Smythe QC again, I'll take the fish any day. The only reason Humphrey's version of "Reality Testing" didn't lose the trust he'd built up is that he hadn't built up any trust.

But many mediators are more subtle. Although they're still wedded to the idea that the way to generate movement is to confront the parties with the opposing arguments, they nevertheless have an inkling that the fish to the face may forfeit all that trust that they've worked so hard to build up. So they confront the parties more subtly, perhaps dressing it up as "helping the parties understand the other side's position". And, yes, that's probably better than the wet fish approach. But I'm afraid it still means the mediator forfeits some of the trust that they've built up. All of a sudden the parties find that the mediator, who they thought empathised, who they thought understood, who seemed to be affirming their position, actually doesn't and isn't, because the mediator appears to think the other side's position has some merit too.

Moreover, most people's response to being confronted with an opposing case is to push back. If there are lawyers in the room, they can't help themselves. For them, it's a reflex. And, in fairness, they're being paid for precisely that reflex. So they offer an immediate rebuttal of anything the mediator says that might be viewed as an attack on their client's position. "Ah, yes, but, we can answer that, because……" And which plays better in the client's head? The mediator, tentatively putting forward the arguments of the other side, whose position the disputant knows to be *morally wrong* and *legally flawed*, because that's what the soundtrack in their own head is telling them, or their lawyer's response, confirming, if confirmation were needed, that *truth*, *justice* and *morality* are on their side? I'm afraid that in these circumstances people hear only what they want to hear. Actually, that may not be putting it strongly enough. Perhaps in these circumstances people hear only what they are *able* to hear. What they are *able* to compute. Which is that, as their lawyer has told the mediator, they were *right* all along. Nothing else computes, nothing else makes any sense, since the story they've told themselves internally has already aligned every possible value judgement with their case and their position.

And if the parties don't have a lawyer, they still feel the need to push back, if not in legal terms then in the terms of *morality* and *fairness* in which they have couched their position. And if the parties don't have a lawyer to speak for them, that's almost worse, because the brain can really only pay attention to one narrative at one time, and if someone is either speaking themselves, delivering their own rebuttal of the opposing case, or even just preparing to do so, with their rebuttal already playing in their head whilst they wait for the mediator to stop speaking, there is only one narrative that they're even capable of listening to. Their own. You can try this at home: the next time your spouse, partner or significant other is talking to you, start planning a rebuttal of what they're saying whilst they're still talking. You'll find (a) that you end up listening to your own internal rebuttal in preference to what they are saying, and (b) that you haven't a clue what they actually finished up saying, because by then you were listening to your own internal rebuttal, and (c) that they will divorce you because your eyes will betray you and they will be able to tell that you weren't listening to a word they were saying. So too in a mediation: by the time the party that the mediator has been confronting has first listened to their own rebuttal playing internally and then delivered that rebuttal in response (or listened to their lawyer delivering it) they're convinced that they have decisively rebutted whatever it was that they didn't quite listen to that the mediator said.

But don't the parties need to be told the other side's case? Er, no. They don't. Not normally. My fellow mediators, I promise you that most of the time you don't need to "help the parties understand the other side's position". They know perfectly well what the other side say. That's exactly why they're so upset! A case doesn't usually come to litigation and thereafter to mediation until most avenues short of a trial have been tried. In the inheritance dispute I mediated in London earlier this week the parties had over the course of three years tried a "Family Settlement Meeting" (which turned into a Family Slanging Match, followed by a Family Walk Out), they'd exchanged solicitors' letters, they'd each sacked their solicitors and got new ones to write the same letters all over again, they'd started court proceedings and between them served on each other a Particulars of Claim, a Defence and Counterclaim, a Reply and Defence to Counterclaim, and goodness knows what other court documents. Each side had spent over £100,000 in legal costs, preparing and exchanging witness statements, medical experts' reports, talking to and at their solicitors, and travelling to London to have case conferences with their barristers. They'd produced so many documents between them that I literally couldn't carry the stack of lever arch files that they kindly supplied to me down to London on the train, and I had to send them ahead of me by post. And then, on the evening of the mediation, they exchanged "Position Statements", each running to over ninety paragraphs, which cut and pasted for each other's delectation some of the best points they'd made to each other over the past three years in all the previous documents. These folk don't need "help to understand the other side's case". They've lived and breathed the dispute for the past three years. They could each appear on Mastermind on the specialist subject of My Dispute and What's Wrong With What the Other Side Say. Brother and sister mediators, the idea that anything you might say in the five minutes (at most!) that you might get uninterrupted in a mediation is going to change the view of their case that the parties have formed over hundreds of hours and hundreds of thousands of pounds of legal costs is, well, it's a lovely idea, really it is, but it's simply fanciful.

Nope, even done gently, confronting a party with the other side's case isn't usually necessary, it doesn't move that party one millimetre, and, worse, it generally serves only to re-reinforce each side's position. All of which brings me on to the vexed (and, indeed, vexing) issue of the opening Joint Session. This is what Humphrey Forbes-Smythe QC, with a fine disregard for the notion that he might want to use words that the person he was mediating might actually understand, called a "plenary" session. There is a view in mediation circles that the best – indeed, for some mediators, the *only* – way to start a mediation is with a kind of mini trial, presided over by the mediator at the head of the table, in which each side is given the chance to confront the other with the strength of their case. Yes, I know. Given what I've just said about confrontation in mediation, it doesn't sound a great idea, does it? But there's a lot of people out there who seem to have a lot invested in the idea of opening every mediation with a joint session, so it deserves a section on its own.

The Opening Joint Session

I should begin with a warning. Some of the great and the good of the mediation establishment (or, at any rate, some of those who consider themselves to be the great and the good of the mediation establishment, which probably amounts to the same thing) disagree with every word I'm about to write. Strongly. Violently even, if that weren't a bit unmediatorish. I told you earlier that my view that mediators can and indeed should feel and show empathy is a bit at odds with the conventional view that we need to maintain a detached independence at all times, but that's just a little local difficulty, a mere difference of emphasis, compared to the difference between us on the issue of holding joint sessions to begin mediations.

There are plenty of mediators who take the view that a mediation that doesn't start with a joint session isn't really a mediation at all. I'm not sure what they think it is, but it's definitely not "proper" mediation. I realised just how strongly some mediators are wedded to this notion of holding an opening joint session at every mediation about five years ago, when I invited a newly qualified mediator to join my little mediation business, mediation1st. Now, I need to give you a bit of context here. And some of that context may come as an unwelcome surprise for any mediators just starting out on the mediator's path. I'm sorry about that. But this is true: there are too many mediators in the UK. There may even be more mediators than there are mediations. And every year the Mediation Schools spew out more eager newly qualified mediators. Many, and perhaps even most of whom will never, ever mediate a single case. Which is sad. I suspect that to actually carve out a career as a mediator, on top of acquiring a mediator's qualification, you need to have a certain aptitude for mediation (obviously), a degree of determination to make mediation your career that borders on the obsessive, and a lot of luck. And I attribute any success that I or any of the other mediators at mediation1st have had in the crowded mediation market place to those very factors. We're all hopefully reasonably good mediators, we're definitely obsessed (sorry, did I say obsessed? I meant to say enthused) about mediation, and I think we've all of us been lucky. That's all. But from the outside, there appears to be a perception amongst some would-be mediators that all that's missing to kick-start their mediation careers is getting onto the mediation1st panel. They see a successful mediation provider with busy mediators on its panel and think they'd like some of that. I get that. As a result, we get inundated with applications. All the time. We could have a hundred mediators in a matter of days if we wanted. But, most of the applications, we decline. Politely and regretfully. But we decline them. Partly, because we just don't have the administrative resources to manage a hundred mediators. Partly because what I enjoy doing is mediating, not managing other mediators. Partly because I think the success of the mediation1st "brand"[2] in the market place requires a certain consistency of approach, so that lawyers know that if they instruct any mediator from mediation1st they'll be getting a broadly similar take on the mediation process. What the marketing people call "consistent brand values". And if we had a hundred mediators, that consistency of approach would go out of the window (I think this is what the marketing people call "diluting brand values"). But, mainly, we decline the applications because I don't actually believe that the mediation1st brand is all that these lovely people need to become successful mediators – what they need is the ability, the enthusiasm but above all, the luck – and I can't give them that, and so I don't actually believe that taking them on board the good ship mediation1st would change anything for them.

But, among those hundreds of applications, there was one that I followed up. The chap had impressive credentials on paper. He had come by way of a recommendation from a mutual friend in the mediation world, which impressed me, firstly because I respect her opinion and, secondly, because he had gone to the trouble of getting her to speak to me. And he was based in a part of the country that our mediators can find hard to reach[3], so the idea of a new mediator concentrating on that area had a certain attraction. I was interested. I met him a couple of times. I thought he was a natural mediator, and would be an asset to mediation1st. We seemed to get on. And so I asked him to join our happy band. He was thrilled. At which point, I mentioned the fact that we aim for a certain consistency of approach in the mediation market place, and that part of that consistency of approach involved not forcing the parties to a mediation to have an opening joint session if they didn't want one.

---

2 I speak Marketing fluently.

3 Just about everywhere is hard to reach from Norfolk.

That blew it. If I had said that I expected him to sign our mediator's contract in blood but that before he did so I just needed to reveal to him that mediation1st was actually a cover for a Satanic plot to destroy civilisation, return the world to the Dark Ages, and make all the little children cry, and that to that end we proposed beginning every mediation by sacrificing a kitten, it couldn't have had a worse effect. Our would-be new mediator was simply aghast. He hadn't realised we didn't insist on opening with a joint session! That wouldn't be proper mediation. He simply couldn't in good conscience be associated with an outfit that didn't begin every mediation with a joint session. Generally, he gave me the impression that sacrificing a kitten would have been altogether more acceptable, provided of course that the kitten was sacrificed at a joint session. And that was that. We lost a chap who I thought would make a great mediator. Which was a pity. Worse, I'm not sure if he ever recovered from the shock, because my extensive research (nearly two minutes on a well known search engine) suggests he never did get going as a mediator, which would be a real shame because, as I say, I thought he was a natural.

Now, I know that you, dear reader, are a person blessed with a sharp intellect and sound judgement. Your purchase of this book demonstrates as much. So, you will have noticed that the position that I was espousing wasn't exactly hard-line. I was merely saying that our policy was not to *force* the parties to have a joint session *if they didn't want to have one*. My personal opinion is that the staged confrontation of a joint session as a way to open a mediation is usually unnecessary, unhelpful and counterproductive – for all the reasons that the mediator confronting the parties with the opposing point of view is usually unnecessary, unhelpful and counterproductive. At best it achieves nothing, at worst it entrenches each party in their own position. If there were no constraints to my following my own preference, I'd probably never start a mediation with a joint session. But I wasn't going that far. I know that many Mediation Schools teach the opening joint session as holy writ, and that many if not most mediators hold them. And I know that as a result many lawyers expect them. Sometimes the parties, or more usually their lawyers, come to the mediation with a prepared speech ready for the joint session, and if I don't let them make it, they'll be like a dog whose bone has been taken away for the duration of the mediation. So, right at the outset the mediators at mediation1st discuss with the parties to the dispute whether they want a joint session. That was all that I was proposing. That we discuss it. That we mediators give the parties a choice here. Yet even this modest notion was nevertheless enough to persuade someone who I thought was potentially a talented mediator, and who'd gone to some trouble to get on to the mediation1st panel, that we were a bunch of dangerous radicals with whom he couldn't in good conscience associate.

Why? Why are so many mediators absolutely wedded to starting every mediation with a joint session? I don't know. It's not because of any hard data that shows that mediations that start with a joint session work better than mediations that don't. I've never seen any statistics or figures to that effect. Since the Disciples of the Sacred Joint Session never conduct a mediation without one they logically can't have access to data that might show what happens if they didn't start that way. Whereas at mediation1st, despite my personal view that, actually, I'd rather start most mediations by sticking my head down the loo and flushing it than begin with a joint session, we do give the parties the choice. That's the choice of whether or not to have a joint session, not whether or not the mediator should stick their head down the loo. And occasionally, the parties choose to start with a joint session. Less than 5% of the time, it's true. But sometimes, they do, and as a result we have some experience of both approaches. For example, I can tell you that mediations that start with a joint session will tend to finish later than those that don't. Basically, by the time we've got everyone into the joint room, had a joint session, and then got everyone back into their own rooms, we've probably lost at least half an hour. And then the mediator spends the next hour and a half calming everyone back down and trying to get them back into the pragmatic frame of mind that they were in before the joint session triggered an avalanche of moral or legal certainties on all sides. So, a joint session probably puts the settlement back by a couple of hours. That's not a big deal, but it's so. And I can also tell you that our experience is that mediations that start with a joint session are *less* likely to settle. Now, don't get me wrong. I'm not claiming that our experience of both approaches in some way *proves* that joint sessions don't work and that every mediator ought therefore to accept definitively that it's better to start without one. Like most things in mediation, and indeed in life generally, it's open to debate. I accept that. As I say, my position isn't hard-line here, and there are objections that could be made if I were to suggest that our experience is conclusive on the point. Firstly, I don't know if the mediations that we've conducted at mediation1st constitute a statistically significant sample, especially when the parties choose a joint session in so few of them. Secondly, I have to allow for the possibility that the small minority of our cases that opt for a joint session do so precisely because the parties are actually further apart than those who don't, so that we're not comparing like with like. It's not inherently implausible to wonder whether parties who don't want a ritual confrontation and just want to get on with the negotiation are in fact starting less entrenched than those who are wedded to bashing lumps out of each other with legal argument at a joint session. And, thirdly, I'm guessing that one could argue that the fact that mediators like myself who think an opening joint session is unhelpful don't have as much success with them could be attributable simply to our dislike of opening with a joint session. The mediator may be the problem. I'm not saying those objections would be right, by the way. I'm just acknowledging that our experience that the chances of settlement are higher without a joint session is not (necessarily) conclusive. Though if I were a Disciple of the Sacred Joint Session that experience might nevertheless give me pause for thought. But, to put the point at its very lowest, I am aware of no data – none – that suggests that starting with a joint session increases the chances of settlement.

If there's no empirical evidence that starting with a joint session is a good move, perhaps the common attachment to beginning mediations this way simply reflects the fact that most mediators in the UK are lawyers. As, obviously, are the professions – solicitors, barristers and legal executives – who provide representation at mediations. And perhaps especially in the UK, where we are very proud of our adversarial legal system, we tend to think of the trial as being the apogee of the dispute resolution process. The gowns and the wigs and the fine speeches, the erudite submissions, the incisive cross examination, that's what it's all about, isn't it? And perhaps subconsciously the legal profession – advisors, advocates and mediators, all of us – think of a mediation as a poor man's substitute for the full glory of a trial, and feel that the least we can do is to start the mediation with something that looks a bit like a trial. The parties on opposite sides of the table, the mediator sitting at the head of the table presiding in judge-like fashion over the proceedings, the barristers addressing speeches to the mediator, that's almost as good as a trial, isn't it?

Er, no. It isn't. Sorry. They're different things. You wouldn't say that the great thing about a railway train is that the engine pulls a load of coaches behind it, so it must follow that the best thing an airline could do is to attach a string of railway coaches to the back of its planes, would you? Trains and planes are different. They work differently, and they're aiming to do different things. So too trials and mediations. In a trial the advocate is attempting to persuade an independent third party (that would be the judge) that the legal narrative that they have assembled about a case is preferable to the legal narrative that the other side has put together. To that end, the advocate will emphasise how strong their case is. It's in accordance with *justice*. With the *merits*. With *legal authority*. Of course it is[4]. And in order to persuade the independent third party to side with one's case, it's legitimate, and perhaps even desirable, to denigrate the other side's case. To be (very politely) rude about it. Sometimes, even, to use the most terrible insult permitted in the courts, which is "with respect". As in "With respect to m' learned friend's argument…" which, for any non-lawyers reading this, actually translates as "With total contempt for the argument, if one can dignify it by calling it an argument, of my friend, who clearly isn't as learned as I had thought, and who I met for the first time this morning and who most certainly isn't my friend….". And if after all that the independent third party is persuaded, they will adopt your narrative and give judgement in your favour. Victory!

Whereas in a mediation, there may be an independent third party present (that would be the mediator) but it's not about persuading them. They're not going to give judgement in your favour. They

---

4 No advocate ever put forward their case on the basis that it flew in the face of justice, produced an unfair result and was against all the legal authorities.

couldn't if they wanted to. What's more, persuading the mediator is just about the worst thing you could do. Why? Well, because if the mediator were to allow themselves to be persuaded by one side, the other side would sense it. We can all sense when someone is "against us" even if they try to hide it. It's an ability our forebears learned in prehistory, probably in order to enable them to tell whether that woolly mammoth blocking the path was a threat or not. And if the other side senses that the mediator is against them, and therefore ceases to trust the mediator, then the mediator's ability to generate movement in the other room will be gone at a stroke, they'll be as much use to you in the other side's room as a woolly mammoth would, and you'll have wasted the mediation fee.

A memo to barristers and mediation advocates

So, a memo to all those excellent barristers and other mediation advocates who very kindly address their arguments to me when we (very occasionally) do have joint sessions:

(a) You're addressing the wrong person. I'm not going to be persuaded and I have no power to make a ruling in your favour. You might try talking to the people opposite you. It's them you're negotiating with; and

(b) You don't actually want to persuade me. Really you don't. Trust me on this. Mediation isn't about persuading the mediator of your legal or moral narrative, it's about persuading, or rather, it's about moving, the *other* party; and

(c) The trouble with talking directly to that other party is that they already have *their own* legal and moral narrative, which they've developed, rehearsed and internalised over months and years, and they aren't going to accept yours to replace it in a hurry. However clever you are, and however cleverly you put your points. What you say will doubtless be legally rigorous and morally sound, because you are a very fine advocate[5], but the other side have already internally appropriated all those same values – legal rigour, moral soundness, and the rest – to their position, so your attempt to argue the opposite just won't compute for them. Which means that since attempting to persuade the other side to accept your legal or moral narrative over theirs is a non-starter, then the goal in mediation is simply to persuade them – or maybe, to let the mediator persuade them, because that's actually what you've hired a mediator for – to *move* their negotiating position *despite* their own narrative. And whilst bigging up your own case, and maybe even denigrating the opponent's case may be required in front of a judge, in terms of getting the opposing party to move their position at a mediation, it's totally counterproductive. And, yes, I really mean exactly that. It's not just ineffective, it's counterproductive. *It. Makes. Things. Worse.* I told you earlier that if I've learned one thing in my work as a mediator, it's this: people don't move until they feel that their position and the way they feel about it has been recognised. Why would they move to accommodate someone who doesn't recognise what they say or understand where they are coming from? Such a person's position is almost by definition going to be, from their perspective, *unreasonable*. And when you, dear skilled barrister or mediation advocate, big up your case, or denigrate the opposing party's case at an opening joint session, you might just as well be holding up signs with great big whopping red letters on them which say:

NO, WE DO NOT UNDERSTAND YOUR POSITION. NO, WE DON'T SEE ANY MERIT IN WHAT YOU SAY. AND NO, WE DON'T CARE HOW YOU FEEL ABOUT IT.

And even if you don't actually hold up the signs, all the other side will hear is that message, and I am afraid it will entrench them in their position.

You'd be better off, actually, telling the other side that you do understand their case, that you can see merit in it, that you recognise just how strongly they feel about it, and that plainly the eventual settlement will

---

5   Seriously. Most of the advocates and advisors I come across at mediation are really, really good.

have to take all of that into account. You might even offer an apology for anything your client has done that might be criticised. The difficulty with that approach, which might otherwise actually be constructive, however, is that, unless your own client is an extremely sophisticated user of the mediation process[6] they will then feel that they are not understood by their own advocate, and they in turn will feel upset and entrenched in their position as a consequence. Bigging up the other side's case is not usually what your client pays you good money to do. So that mostly doesn't help either. But the good news is that whilst you may not be in a position to offer the affirmation that might start to open up the other side's negotiation position, you have a mediator on hand who is being paid a handsome mediation fee[7] to go into each room individually to do precisely that. And whilst they can't do it at the joint session, since affirmation offered to one side in front of the other will wind up the other, just as soon as the joint session is over, they'll start doing just that, and we can start to make some progress.

(d) Or, (4). Or (iv). I forget which system we're using, but I think this is still part of my memo to barristers and mediation advocates, and like all the best memos it really ought to have numbered bullet points. Anyhow, fourthly, if I were an advocate at a mediation where a joint session is taking place, I'd restrict myself to pleasantries, and I would most definitely not deploy my best points against the other side in that joint session. Why? Well, let me share with you something I've noticed in mediations. Imagine, if you will, a mediation where the Defendant thinks that they have a particularly strong argument that clause 5.4 of the contract between the parties means the Claimant's case case must fail. If that point is explained to me, as mediator, there may come a point in the Claimant's room where I may be able to say to the Claimant and their advisors, in private, in confidence, and without confrontation: "So, the Defendant is talking to me about clause 5.4, is there an issue on that?" And, if I have been successful in building trust in the Claimant's room, and if I have judged the moment right – and

---

6   Some insurers, for example, attend so many mediations and have become so sophisticated that they may be happy to go along with this approach because they understand that it may help the process.

7   Thank you very much.

that's kind of my job, judging the moment – the Claimant's advisor may just acknowledge an element of risk: "Well, yes, we recognise that may be an area where there's a bit of risk for us". And, a bit of risk is all I need to work with (more on that in chapter five). But, that's *only* if the Defendant hasn't made the point at an opening joint session. I've noticed that if the Defendant makes the point at the joint session, the Claimant won't listen to it. Not at any point in the mediation. Chances are, the Claimant's advocate will ask to reply at the opening session, and will say "The point about clause 5.4 is a total non-point because….". Or, when I come into their room, they won't even give me time to say "What are your thoughts on the joint session?" before they're telling me "The point from the joint session about clause 5.4 is a total non point because….". And here's the thing. If I try to go back to that point in the Claimant's room, later on, when the trust has been built, and when I judge the moment to be right, it doesn't have any impact. When I say, "So, the Defendant is talking to me about clause 5.4, is there an issue on that?" the response will be "Yes, but that's a total non-point because as we already said….". And then I haven't got that element of doubt to work with. It's almost as if that point, having been initially made in the hostile environment of a joint session, is thereafter labelled, in the brains of the Claimant and their advisors, with something like "Hostile point – not compatible with our narrative – does not compute – not to be listened to – to be rebutted immediately when raised". And for the rest of the mediation the point carries that label, as it were, and its force is lost. Why? Is there some neurological reason that explains this phenomenon in terms of how our brains process or store information? I have no idea. That's way above my pay grade. If there's anyone out there reading this who can explain it, please get in touch. I'd be interested. For now, I'm just sharing what I have observed, which is that making a point in the adversarial environment of a joint session can mean losing the impact of the point in the other room for the rest of the mediation. Which is why, were I an advocate at a joint session, I'd keep my powder very much dry, and maybe concentrate on priming the mediator to raise my best points at the appropriate moment in a less adversarial context.

So, then, what *can* you usefully do or say at an opening joint session?

Search me. I don't know. As far as I can see there's almost nothing that can usefully be said by anyone at an opening joint session in order to progress the mediation. Sorry. But then, I'm not the one advocating the holding of an opening joint session in each and every mediation.

End of memo to barristers and other mediation advocates.

What about Transformative Mediation?

Some very clever bears have drawn a distinction between "Problem Solving Mediation" and "Transformative Mediation". Sometimes a broadly similar distinction is drawn between "Commercial Mediation" and "Transformative Mediation". Problem Solving (or Commercial) Mediation[8] may not be concerned with the relationship between the parties at all. I've mediated no end of disputes between businesses that all came down, essentially, to one question: what's the right price for this? That was the problem to be solved. And all the parties needed to agree was an answer to that problem: a figure that both sides could live with. The relationship between the parties may have been as broken at the end of the mediation as at the start (or it may not). They may have left without having seen each other once during the course of the mediation (if we didn't have an opening session) or they may have parted with a handshake and a smile. But, the relationship wasn't the point. They had a problem, which was that they couldn't agree the amount to be written on a cheque, and once that problem was sorted they can both move on, stop wasting time and cost on the dispute, and get back to their lives or businesses.

Transformative Mediation, however, is actually concerned with the underlying relationship. It's about how the parties get on. The theory of Transformative Mediation says that the dispute can actually be about a breakdown in the way the parties interact, and views the transformation of the interaction as the main thing – more important than the terms of the settlement, or even whether there is a "settlement" as such. And I'm

---

8 For our present purposes, we can treat the two terms as the same, though they're not identical in all respects.

told that there are practitioners of Transformative Mediation who take the view that, as it's all about the interaction, getting the parties together in joint session – at the outset and potentially throughout the mediation – is what it's all about.

That's fine by me. I have huge respect for transformative mediators and what they do. Ladies, gentlemen, I doff my mediator's hat in your general direction. And I'm certainly not about to fall out with you over joint sessions. Indeed, since I've never been instructed on the basis that the settlement doesn't matter, and that it's all about the interaction, I guess that means that I (along, I suspect, with most commercial mediators in the UK) don't get asked to do Transformative Mediation. So it would be pretty rich of me to start telling you folks what you should and shouldn't do. Your field, your expertise, your call. Go, transformative mediators, go!

But although those clever bears have – rightly – drawn an important distinction between Problem Solving Mediation on the one hand and Transformative Mediation on the other, in practice I suspect the distinction isn't always that clear. Not one person who has instructed mediation1st has ever specified that they want either a problem solving mediator or a transformative mediator. People come to us with a host of stuff. With a dispute. A court case. An issue. An argument. A thing. Last year I drove through the flat lands and broad skies of the Fens to mediate what was described to us as "a thing in Peterborough". And a slippery, amorphous and hard to define thing it was too. But no one has ever come to us with a mediation that either was or wasn't specified as transformative.

I suspect that most mediations fall somewhere on a spectrum. At one end, there are cases that plainly are simply problems to be solved: those cases which boil down to a figure, to "Who Pays Whom How Much?" Though even there, an underlying relationship may, or may not, be improved. Somewhere in the middle of the spectrum are those disputes between family members who have fallen out over their inheritance from Aunt Edna, or between former partners who have fallen out over their respective shares in what was once their dream home. At one level, these folk simply have a problem that needs solving. How do we divide Aunt Edna's estate? How do we share the proceeds of the dream home? At another level, a relationship break down is likely to be a part of the background to the problem, and the resolution of the problem may, or may not, impact on that broken relationship. Still further towards the transformative end of the spectrum are those disputes between neighbours who live cheek by jowl, and whose dispute may be articulated in terms of a problem that definitely needs solving – typically the location of a boundary or the operation of a right of way – but where the interaction between them may very much be part of the problem to be solved. Then, I'm guessing that Divorce Mediation, (which tends to be referred to by the rather more user friendly name of Family Mediation), and which I don't do, also falls somewhere towards the transformative end of the spectrum. In Divorce or Family Mediation there's a problem (or rather, there's a lot of problems) to be sorted out, for sure (Who gets the house? Who gets the children? Who gets the budgerigar?) but particularly where there are children whom the parties will be co-parenting, improving the relationship between the parties, at least so as to enable civil communication about who picks little Amanda up after violin practice, might also be a consummation devoutly to be wished. And right at the far end of the spectrum may be those cases that are properly characterised as pure Transformative Mediations, where it really is all about the interaction between the parties. For example, I'm guessing that there would be instances of workplace mediation, where two employees just can't work together, or community mediation, where it really is all about transforming the interaction.

Now, I've conceded that if the folk who do Transformative Mediation tell me that they need to start with a joint session, or even spend most or all of the mediation in a joint session, I'm in no position to disagree, and indeed I haven't the slightest desire to disagree. I've been talking about Problem Solving Mediation, which is what most commercial mediators in the UK do, and where in my view an opening joint session is usually about as much use as a waterproof teabag. But if mediation is a spectrum, that leaves the question: at what point along the spectrum does the opening joint session become potentially useful?

I don't know. Probably it's not an exact point. Each case is different. But my instinct is that (perhaps leaving the specialist field of Family Mediation, on which I don't comment either way, to one side) so long as there is a defined problem apart from the relationship that needs solving – how do we divide our inheritance from Aunt Edna, for example – then a joint session at the outset isn't going to help a lot even where the interaction between the parties could be improved as well. And that's because each party will have developed their own internal narrative full of moral and legal judgements as to why they and not the other person ought to have Aunt Edna's silver spoons (or whatever) and a joint session at which they hurl those value judgements at each other will be thoroughly counterproductive in so far as solving the problem goes, for all the reasons I've already set out, and is likely to be counter-productive in terms of improving the relationship too. Which would mean that it's only in those cases that really are right at the transformative end of the spectrum where opening with a joint session may (so the Transformative Mediators tell me) be helpful. Otherwise, my view would be that generally it's better to start without a joint session.

Does that mean that in the majority of the cases that commercial mediators see, where there is a problem to be solved, I'm giving up on improving the parties' relationship? That it's only about solving the problem? No. Not at all. I've seen time and time again that even in what one might call Problem Solving Mediation the relationship between the parties can be improved without each side confronting the other with their arguments and value judgements at a joint session (which does nothing to solve the problem and nothing to improve the relationship anyway). Remember, the dispute wasn't about the arguments deployed, any more than trial by combat was about the weapons used. The parties simply pulled the arguments and value judgements into the positions they needed them to be in to match their own opposing interests. And as long as those interests remain opposed, that's precisely the positions the arguments will stay in: opposed. But when those interests are reconciled, when the parties have agreed how to share Aunt Edna's silver spoons, and their interests are no longer opposed because they've settled the dispute then, sometimes, if the relationship matters enough, and the parties' hearts are in the right place, and the stars are too, something magical happens. The parties are reconciled. The arguments cease to matter. Without the fixed points of the now settled dispute to anchor all those legal arguments and moral certainties in the cinders of the world, they just float away. And a sister who just a few hours ago refused even to be in the same building as the "bitch-cow from hell" that was her sibling asks to see her "dear lost sister", and confides to her mediator that "Of course, I do understand that she had a point of view too".

The other side had a point of view too? Well, blow me down with a feather. Who'd have thought that? And all without a joint session.

Keeping an open mind

If you're still reading this, and haven't cast my little book onto your fire on the grounds that you can't in good conscience give houseroom to a book that doesn't advocate holding a joint session at the beginning of every mediation then thank you for staying with me. Thanks for having an open mind. And I suppose that an open mind is really all I'm asking for.

I recognise that there are people out there to whom an opening joint session is really, really important. People who get (to me, inexplicably) worked up about not holding one. And I'm not saying that it's never appropriate. I've conceded that if transformative mediators think it's appropriate for their work, then I shouldn't knock that, and I don't. Ditto matrimonial mediators. Even in other cases, I acknowledge that there may be instances where the lawyers or their clients are so wedded to making speeches to each other that it would cause more problems than it solves to deny them the opportunity. And I entirely accept that there may sometimes be a case for having, if not a full-blown opening session where each side is confronted with the legal arguments of the other, at least an opening "meet and greet" session where all can smile politely and shake hands. Sometimes.

It's not as if I *never* hold a joint session. I give the parties the choice, in private session, as to whether they want a joint session. You may of course ask: what happens if one side wants one and the other doesn't? What then? Well, when I put the choice to the parties I explain that if both sides want a joint session, then we'll have one, but that if even one side doesn't want one then it's likely to be counterproductive, and that in those circumstances we need to look for other ways for the parties' points to be got across. And the parties are usually fine with that.

But of course, the issue of one side wanting a joint session when the other doesn't mostly doesn't arise, because, in the overwhelming majority of cases, over 95% of cases in our experience at mediation1st, if given the choice, *neither* party wants a joint session. Of course they don't! The clue is in the fact that they've come to mediation. They don't want conflict. Most people don't. They don't want a trial. Or a mini trial, thank you very much. They don't even want to sit opposite their opponent. They probably don't even want to see them. That, partly, is *why they've come to mediation instead of going to a trial.*

Brother and sister mediators, you may not share my view of the usefulness or otherwise of joint sessions. And that's fine. We're all different, we all have our own mediation style, and there's nothing wrong with that. All I'm suggesting is that we give the parties, our clients, the choice, and I'd just ask you to consider this. If the parties themselves don't want the confrontation that going to court would entail, if they've come to mediation precisely in order to avoid that confrontation, if they're willing to make concessions, to give up or to pay money to avoid the confrontation, how clever is it if the first thing that so many mediators do, right at the start of the mediation, is to tell the parties that they're going to have to begin with the very confrontation that they were hoping to avoid and to sit right opposite the very people they were hoping not to see? Is that really how we see our role as mediators? To start every mediation by making 95% of our clients do something they really don't want to do? Something they were prepared to take a financial hit to avoid? How effective is overruling our clients' preferences likely to be in enabling us to build the trust that will ultimately help to generate movement in the mediation?

Come to that, and I concede that this is a different point, how effective is overruling our clients' preferences going to be in helping us develop our mediation practices?

Mediators in the UK have an annual conference. I try to go when I can, though often I'm too busy mediating. But at the last conference I did attend I almost had a row with a very eminent barrister. I say "almost' because although he seemed to me to be spoiling for a fight, I just smiled as sweetly as I could and said "Is that so?" to everything he said, which had the twin advantages that (a) we didn't have a row, and (b) it wound him up even more. The subject he wanted to fight about was, and you'll have guessed it, the joint session. What I do in not holding joint sessions, he said, was "not proper mediation". He wouldn't stand for it: if he were mediating, he'd jolly well make the parties "do it properly and have a joint session, whether they want it or not". The only problem with that was, as he admitted ruefully, that despite his great eminence, no one seemed to want to instruct him to mediate for them in the first place, which he just couldn't understand.

I wonder, what reason could there possibly be?

CHAPTER FIVE

Not always so

As someone who is lucky enough to earn my living as a mediator, my objection to much in the way of confrontation in mediation is essentially pragmatic. It doesn't work. It reinforces parties in their opposing positions. It sends them back into the trenches.

From a Zen perspective, the difficulties caused by confronting the parties to a mediation with the other side's moral or legal narrative can be explained in terms of the Buddha's Noble Truths. Noble Truths numbers One to Three were that life is just not satisfactory, that it simply won't comply (for long) with the stories we tell ourselves about how it *should* be, and that the first step to dealing with this situation is to begin to *accept the world as it actually is*. When you think about it, confronting the parties with the other side's mental narrative isn't actually doing anything at all about accepting the world as it is. It's just more of the same. We see (correctly) that the parties are prevented by their own mental narrative of how the world *should* be from reaching a settlement, so we offer them…..an opposing narrative of how the world *should* be. And all we end up doing is fighting about the meaning of terms, about the *shoulds* and the *oughts* and the *rights* and the *wrongs*, and who can better apply them to their own case. That's never going to work. We're in a hole, and the Zen approach to holes, pragmatic as always, is pretty much that the first thing to do when you're in a hole, is to stop digging. The point is to *accept the world as it is*, not to promote one narrative of how it *should* be in opposition to another.

Which raises the question: how is the world, then?

Well, the Buddha had a lot to say on that subject. More than we can possibly fit into what is supposed to be a book about Mediation. We need a bit of a summary here. So, let me tell you about a talk by a Zen teacher that I went to listen to in London. The teacher was a monk from Japan, and he told us a story about one of the Zen Masters of old who said that the whole of the Buddha's teaching could be condensed *into just two words*:

Not….

always…

so.

How we Buddhist students in the audience laughed. Inwardly, of course. We were far too polite to laugh out loud. No doubt "Not always so" may be two words in Japanese, but how ironic that this wise, wise man, for all his wisdom, hadn't spotted that "Not always so" is actually three words in English! Afterwards over a cup of tea we had a giggle, and several of us decided that "Everything changes" would work just as well. And it's two words! Clever, no? I was on the train back to Norfolk before it hit me that this wise, wise man, who spoke several languages better than I speak one, could almost certainly count to three, and that he was just demonstrating this very point to us: everything changes. Even the number of words required to say "Not always so" is, er, well, not always so.

At any rate, "not always so" is how the Buddha saw the world. It's changing. All the time. Nothing is certain. Nothing is forever. That's why the world won't comply with the stories we tell ourselves about how it *should* be for long. The world is in flux. What's more, we can't predict where or what state it's fluxing to with any certainty. And when it reaches that state, whatever it is, it'll just flux on. Life, the first three Noble Truths tell us, complies neither with our predictions nor our predilections. All of which is actually a rather modern idea. You'll recall T E Hulme's "modernist" vision of the world as wind blown cinders that won't stay in one place under the grid of our language. The Buddha would have understood that vision, though I wonder if he might have expressed it slightly differently. His point would perhaps have been that the cinders of the world won't stay in one place long enough to comply with our wishes.

Schrödinger's Cat and Probability Waves

Modern physics too confirms the changing and unpredictable nature of the world. Physicists tell us that change and unpredictability are hard-wired into the universe. In their work they see not certainties but probabilities. The Austrian quantum physicist, Erwin Schrödinger is famous for a thought experiment that involved putting a cat in a sealed box with a radioactive element, a Geiger counter, and a bottle of poison. The radioactive element has an exactly 50% chance of decaying in a set period of time. If it decays, the Geiger counter will detect the decay, and smash the bottle of poison, thereby killing the cat. Only once we open the box at the end of the time period can we see whether the cat is alive or dead. Now, before we go any further, relax. It's a thought experiment. That's all. No actual cats were harmed in Schrödinger's thought experiment. Nor indeed in the writing of this book. There may have been a moment when I came quite close, after our fat cat, Zazen, deleted a sizeable chunk of chapter two by sitting on the computer keyboard, but the moment passed, and Zaza is still very much with us. I've often heard Schrödinger's thought experiment being used as a way to illustrate a proposition that will be familiar to anyone who has either (a) spent several years acquiring a degree in Physics, or alternatively (b) who has devoted half an hour to watching any episode of Doctor Who. The proposition in question is that in Quantum Theory a subatomic particle exists in all possible states at once until it is observed, and so we can't be certain which state we will observe it in. Before it is observed, it may be best understood as a probability wave, reflecting the probability of it being in each possible state, which probability wave collapses into a fixed state at a fixed time at the moment of observation. This model of Quantum Physics is known as the Copenhagen Interpretation, and was developed by Neils Bohr and Werner Heisenberg in the 1920s, in what appears to be an extraordinary coincidence, in Copenhagen. Schrödinger's thought experiment, it is often said, postulates that at the point of opening the box, the cat is a probability wave which is 50% alive and 50% dead, which wave collapses as we look into the box to find kitty either safe and well or dearly departed.

Actually, our friend Schrödinger was trying to demonstrate the opposite point, which was that even before we look into the box the cat is obviously either (a) alive, or (b) dead and that the notion that the box contains a half dead half alive feline probability wave is silly. And no doubt it is silly, though the fact that his thought experiment is widely held to be an exposition of the Copenhagen Interpretation perhaps illustrates the reality that the statements of most quantum physicists have a 50% chance of being understood and a 50% chance of being completely incomprehensible. They too exist as a probability wave, half-baked and half not baked, until some poor student tries to understand them, at which point the probability wave collapses and the student says either "Oh, I see" or "Come again?[1]". Anyhow, whilst modern Quantum Theory remains wedded to the model of subatomic particles being understood as probability waves that collapse into a particular state when observed, answering the question that Schrödinger was addressing, namely whether and how far quantum effects in fact operate beyond the subatomic level, would rapidly get us into seriously deep waters. There are some controversial ideas out there, but insofar as I understand it at all, which isn't very far, there seems to be general agreement that although quantum effects may still operate beyond the subatomic level, they are much harder to observe, which is why you didn't encounter a probability wave the last time you popped out for a pint of milk, and why Schrödinger's cat is in fact either alive or dead, but not 50% both when the box is opened [2].

Well, general agreement or not, I have news for the quantum physicists of this world, and I confidently await the award of my Nobel Prize for Physics upon publication of this little book. Folks, you've got it wrong. Probability waves aren't only to be perceived at a quantum level. The Copenhagen Interpretation also applies to any piece of contested litigation you care to name, none of which exist remotely at a quantum

---

1 I am allowed to say this about physicists because I am married to one.

2 Not only am I married to a physicist but my editor at Law Brief Publishing, Garry, is a theoretical physicist. What are the chances, hey? Anyone less well adjusted could get paranoid. Anyhow, Karen and Garry tell me that all of that paragraph was something of an oversimplification, but that it's probably ok in the context of a book about mediation. Phew.

level[3]. Litigation is neither a "winner" nor a "loser" – not until the point when the judge pronounces. Until then, it too is a probability wave, a percentage chance of winning and a percentage chance of losing, which probability wave collapses as the judge hands down judgement. Sometimes, the probability wave isn't the only thing that collapses as judgement is given.

Einstein resisted the notion that the universe is ultimately random, saying that "God does not play dice"; Stephen Hawking said that Einstein was wrong and that God not only plays dice but "he sometimes throws them where they cannot be seen". The existence of a creator of the universe, let alone their dice playing proclivities, is off limits for this book. But I've seen enough litigation to know that to litigate is to throw the dice, and what's more, to throw them in a darkened room whilst blindfolded and paying for the privilege.

Risk in Litigation

For the lawyers reading this book, I imagine that I don't have to justify the statement above that litigation is a risky business any further. Is litigation risky? Is the Dalai Lama Buddhist? But for any non-lawyers, I've tried throughout this book to avoid asking you to take stuff on trust, so perhaps I need to say a word or two on this. For the lawyers amongst you, you can skip this section. Or you can read it and nod sagely whilst muttering "Yes, I know that" at regular intervals. A word of warning, though: if you're reading this book on public transport, you may want to consider not repeatedly muttering "Yes, I know that" out loud, just in case the person next to you happens to be carrying a wet fish, and gets so irritated that they feel an uncontrollable urge to slap you with it.

One can reach the conclusion that litigation is risky simply by accepting the First Noble Truth. Life is dukkha. It's unsatisfactory. Shit happens. Even if your case is *right*, and *fair*, and in accordance with *Justice*, there's always the risk, in a world of dukkha, that Justice will miscarry. And if you want a bit more detail on just how that might happen, I can

---

3   Definitely nothing subatomic about the legal costs.

do no better than refer you to the great wisdom of Sir Gavin Lightman, QC. The Honourable Mr Justice Lightman was a High Court judge until his retirement in 2008. He's also a qualified Arbitrator, and a Mediator. In 2009 he was elected the President of the Association of European Judges Committed to Mediation. In short, he is about as eminent as one can get, without actually dying. And in 2003 he gave a brilliant speech in which he set out all the reasons why litigation is so very risky.

He stated that: firstly, witnesses can find the whole business of giving evidence so stressful that they "misfire" in the witness box. Secondly, human nature being what it is, a judge can form a completely different view of a witnesses' credibility from the one you expected, believing someone who you think is obviously lying or mistaken, and failing to believe someone whom you just know is telling the truth. Thirdly, in cases involving specialist expertise, the judge, not being an expert in the field, may nevertheless have to decide between two or more expert witnesses, both of whom are specialists, and who know much more about the issue in question than the judge who is deciding between them, which has to be an utterly unsatisfactory way to come to a decision. Then, unexpected documents can come to light at the last moment and totally change one's assessment of a case. The law could change at the last moment too. And barristers and judges, being human (contrary to the popular perception) can have good days, and bad days, and make mistakes. Throw all of that into the mix and, yes, litigation is throwing the dice, blindfolded, and in a darkened room. I've never met a litigator who can't regale you with stories of how they won cases that they never should have won, and if they're honest enough, or drunk enough, most will concede that they also lost cases that they were confident of winning. Which is why Mr Justice Lightman said that experienced trial lawyers had told him that when asked to put a percentage figure on a case's chances of success, they wouldn't give even the strongest cases – what they described as "sure certs" – more than an eighty per cent chance of succeeding.

I don't imagine for one moment that someone as eminent as Sir Gavin Lightman QC would ever need to read my little book but if I may nevertheless address my remarks in your general direction for a moment, Sir, I owe you a debt of gratitude. Over the fifteen years that I've been a mediator I've referred many a litigant and their advisors to your speech and invited them to find it online and read it during a mediation, and the realisation that even a "sure cert" case has a chance of going wrong has played its part in several successful mediations.

Mostly, though, I haven't actually needed to refer litigants to the learned judge's thoughts. The notion that *regardless* of where those concepts of *right* and *wrong*, and all the rest, may be located, the outcome of litigation in an imperfect world, in an imperfect court system, presided over by an imperfect judge and populated by imperfect lawyers and imperfect witnesses may be, well, imperfect – and therefore uncertain – is one to which people are pretty receptive. Brother and sister mediators, we mostly don't have to confront the parties with the other side's case. We don't have to beat them around the head with the arguments that *right* and *wrong* and *law* and *justice* are located somewhere other than where they say they are. That's counterproductive. It's also usually unnecessary. Most people know already that life is uncertain and prone to be unsatisfactory, and litigation doubly so. No one gets to the age where they might be a party to a mediation without knowing that. Even those who (inexplicably) don't support Norwich City will have learned that things don't always turn out as they should. And if we mediators can just resist challenging the parties about where the concepts of *right* and *wrong* and all the rest are located, and thereby triggering a tsunami of moral and legal certainties in response, we'll find that actually people already know the First Noble Truth (as it applies to litigation). They're certain about where *right* and *wrong* lie, but they also know that whether a given piece of litigation will locate them correctly is nevertheless uncertain. They may be confident that Justice *should* be on their side, but they're not confident that Justice won't get it wrong on the day of the trial. And once they've accepted this uncertainty principle in litigation, they'll be able to move on and, yes, even to talk about settlement. That, you will remember, was the Third Noble Truth – that if we can *accept the world as it is* – and that it doesn't comply with all those stories we tell ourselves about how it *should* be – we can start to get unstuck. The Buddha, you'll recall, didn't offer to solve any of the problems presented to him by the man with the 83 problems. His offer was to help the man with the 84th problem, which was coming to terms with, and accepting, the existence of the first 83 problems.

Reframing

So, the role of the mediator is not to challenge the parties to the dispute over who is *right* and who is *wrong*, or what would be *fair* and what would be *unfair*. We can leave their mental narrative about where those value judgements are to be located entirely intact. The truth is, it's going to remain intact whether we leave it alone or not, so there are no points to be won, and there's a lot of time to be wasted, and a lot of trust to be lost, by banging our heads against the wall of their moral or legal positions. Instead, the mediator's role is to help the parties to accept the world as it is. To come to terms with the fact that despite all their certainties about *right* and *wrong*, the outcome of the litigation remains uncertain. To reframe their attitude to the litigation: no longer viewing it in terms of a clash between competing value judgements but simply as a proposition which, in an uncertain world of *dukkha*, carries risk. I think this notion of reframing the terms in which the dispute is perceived, and, indeed, expressed, is so important, so central to what a mediator does, that I've given it a section on its own, even if it's a short section, because it's a short point. But I promise you, it's often the action of reframing the terms in which the dispute is expressed that is the key to generating movement in a mediation. This bit's important.

As we have already observed, so long as the dispute has not been reframed and the parties see and express that dispute in terms of clashing moral or legal certainties, they are almost denying themselves permission to compromise. Compromise involves concessions and if my case is *good*, is *right*, is *lawful* and *just*, and all the rest, then it's difficult to see how I can or should make concessions. Justice herself, trumpet tongued, would plead against the deep damnation of the proposed concessions, and heaven's cherubim, horsed upon the sightless couriers of the air, would blow the horrid compromise in every eye, that tears would drown the wind! Oops. Sorry. Got a bit carried away there[4]. But that's kind of the point. So long as the dispute is defined in terms of *good, bad, fair, unfair, just, unjust,* and all the rest, then those very terms will bring with them a whole load of personal and cultural baggage that all too often will come crashing through the walls of our judgement and carry us away to a place where compromise is unthinkable. And as long as the dispute is expressed in those terms, that place is where the mediation will remain stuck.

Whereas once the dispute is perceived and expressed not in terms of moral or legal certainties, but simply as a risk-bearing proposition in an imperfect world, it's altogether easier for the parties to compromise. Movement then isn't undermining anyone's moral position. It's just a rational, commercial acknowledgement of the risk that derives from the imperfect nature of life. 'Tis but the way of the world, my friends.

What's more, once the litigation is reframed in terms of risk and reward/loss, the parties not only have permission, if you like, to settle, but their positions will inherently contain a degree of flexibility. Moral or legal certainties are, well, they're certain. Set in stone. Frame the dispute in terms of moral or legal propositions and it's going to remain stuck. *Good* will always be *good, right* will always be *right,* and *lawful* will always be *lawful.* Whereas risk, by its very nature, is uncertain. That's rather the point about risk: it's a percentage chance. An assessment of uncertainty. Which will always be, er, uncertain. Fluid. And therefore expressing a case in terms of risk usually permits a degree of flexibility.

So, then, once we've affirmed the parties' respective positions and thereby established trust, what we need to do to start to generate movement is to draw out the parties' knowledge that the litigation comes with risk attached and then to reframe the dispute in terms of that risk and the potential reward/loss that comes with that risk. At that point, we'll find that the question as to how far people will compromise ceases to be about how willing they are to shift their moral perspective

---

4 Zen doesn't really do heaven's cherubim, whether or not horsed on the sightless couriers of the air.

(usually not very far, for they are moral beings) but turns instead on just how risk averse the parties are. Easy, no?

Well, no. There's a danger of trying to go too fast here. As I've said, most people are in general terms receptive to the notion that litigation involves risk. The mediator is often pushing at a bit of an open door here. But, caveat mediator. Whilst the parties may in general terms be receptive to the notion of risk, it's best if the notion that the case under discussion carries risk doesn't originate too obviously with the mediator. If the mediator tries too hard to lead the discussion onto risk him or herself, there's a danger that parties may perceive that the mediator is making a value judgement on their case, and trust might be lost. But, don't worry. There's normally help available to shift the mediation onto a discussion of risk.

Step forward the unsung heroes and heroines of the mediation process.

Step forward the lawyers.

Yes, you read that right. Step forward the lawyers.

A fanfare for the common lawyer

It's fair to say that the legal profession don't always get a good press. We (and, yes, I confess it, I'm a lawyer too) aren't much loved.

> *What do you call a hundred dead lawyers at the bottom of the sea? A good start.*
>
> *What do Father Christmas and an honest lawyer have in common? Neither of them exist.*
>
> *Why won't sharks attack lawyers? Professional courtesy.*

Ho ho ho. I was once at a production of Shakespeare's Henry VI (Part 2) where the audience greeted the line:

> *"The first thing we do, let's kill all the lawyers"*

with cheers and applause. Being a lawyer felt rather lonely and persecuted at that moment. Not that I'm expecting your sympathy (unless you happen to be a lawyer yourself, in which we could have a collective wallow in self pity). But for everyone else, we lawyers aren't likely to be objects of sympathy because whatever people say about us, they reckon that we can console ourselves with our big fat fees, and hug those close to us through the long lonely nights. And it's not just the fact that our fees are fat that gets lawyers a bad name. In the popular perception, lawyers make those fat fees out of the misery of others. There's a Victorian etching you may have seen which shows two rather scrawny individuals fighting over a cow. One is pulling the cow towards him from the front; the other is pulling the cow in the opposite direction from the rear. Sitting in the middle, milking the cow, is a rather ugly fat fellow. The two scrawny individuals fighting over the cow are marked *Claimant* and *Defendant*. The cow has the word *Litigation* on its back. And the ugly fat fellow milking the litigation for his own benefit, yes, he's *The Lawyer*.

One of the joys of being a mediator is that one gets to visit countless solicitors' offices across the length and breadth of the country. And I kid you not, I've been to more than one where a print of this etching is proudly displayed in the boardroom or in the library or even, on a couple of occasions, in the clients' waiting room. As we say in Norfolk: thas a rummun[5]! What possesses lawyers to put a print in their own waiting room that shows them fleecing their clients? Is it some kind of peculiar double bluff, where they think displaying it shows that they're not like that? Do they just think it looks sort of old and lawyerly? Have they not thought about it at all? Ok, this isn't my field. I'm just a mediator who practices a bit of Zen on the side. Or maybe I'm a Zen student who mediates a bit on the side. Either way, marketing and client relations and all that clever modern stuff aren't really my bag. But this still seems to me to be the marketing equivalent of an airline advertising its services with a series of photos of plane crashes.

Which perhaps suggests that we lawyers are often at least partly to blame for our unfavourable public image. And we're also often the first

---

5 This is exceedingly difficult to understand.

to run each other down. When a group of mediators get together, one of their first topics of conversation (right after the one about why they don't get more instructions to mediate) is how little they think of the lawyers who do instruct them. You may think that there might be a link between the first and the second topic. Anyway, perhaps I've just been lucky. Perhaps my experience is atypical. But on the whole, the solicitors, barristers and legal executives whose cases I've mediated are great. Really great. Yes, honestly.

No, of course, they're not perfect. But then, I'm not the perfect mediator either, so in that respect we're a good fit. But I have no doubt that the overwhelming majority of them are motivated by nothing other than the best interests of their clients. The idea that they would seek to milk the litigation for their own benefit, like the fat fellow in the Victorian etching, would be anathema to them. If settlement is right for their client, they'll do what they can to bring that settlement about, and I don't believe that the thought that by doing so they're depriving themselves of the fees they would have made from continuing the litigation even enters their heads.

I've mediated over a thousand cases, and since each case has at least two lawyers, one on each side, and several have more than two, it must follow that I've mediated two to three thousand lawyers. And I can count the instances where I thought a lawyer was trying to prevent a settlement taking place on the fingers of one hand. Well, on the four fingers and one thumb of one hand, to be precise. The occasions when this happened are so few that each one of them sticks in my mind.

There was the solicitor in the North West who simply would not let three brothers settle an inheritance dispute even on what were clearly advantageous terms.

There was a barrister in Bristol who had so little grasp of the mediation process that she treated me as the advocate for the other side throughout, and insisted on referring to the opposing party, who had their own lawyers, as "your clients" when speaking to me.

There was a QC in London (for any non-lawyers, that's a very senior and seriously clever barrister) who effectively dismissed me halfway through a mediation: for all her cleverness she simply could not grasp that everything she said and did was viewed as toxic by the other side, and therefore could not accept that there might be any reason why I wasn't keen to let her speak to them.

Then there was the barrister in a Midlands partnership dispute who quite simply browbeat his poor client into fighting (moral: never trust someone whose every utterance begins with "I'm not looking for fees here, but...").

And lastly there was the barrister who spent the entire mediation complaining about the facilities (the coffee wasn't hot enough, the room wasn't cold enough, the lunch wasn't big enough) and who then threw what can only be described as a temper tantrum when the opposition responded to his client's first offer with a counter-offer rather than an immediate acceptance. A tantrum he threw without even waiting to find out what his client thought about the offer, or how his client wanted to respond.

So, yes, lawyers who prevent settlement, or who at the least make it less likely, do exist. And, no, none of those cases settled. I learned later that the brothers took the inheritance dispute to trial, where their barrister (who wasn't at the mediation) told them at the doors of court that they had no option but to do a deal. A deal that cost them almost exactly twice as much as the deal that their solicitor wouldn't let them do at the mediation. The barrister who thought I was the advocate for the other side got to take her case to trial. There she met the real advocate for the other side, who, I'm told, demolished her case. The QC who effectively dismissed me mid-mediation nevertheless graciously allowed me to stay long enough to witness the success of her strategy of talking directly to the opposition, which was that the opposition packed up and left. As I write this, I don't know the final outcome in the case with the barrister who insisted his client fought a partnership dispute, nor in the case with the barrister who threw a temper tantrum. But, the solicitor who acted in the last case is someone for whom I have a high regard, and if I were a betting man (which I'm not) I'd put my money on her having picked up the phone to her opponent over the next few days and having done a deal directly between solicitors once the emotionally challenged barrister was out of the way. Which would be great, and in its own way a result for the mediation process too, even if the final conclusion didn't involve the mediator. What matters is that the clients get the deal they need, not that the mediator gets to put another notch on their flip chart[6].

And, yes, five cases is five too many. I don't minimise how bad those five cases were. I'm not blind to how much cost and how much upset those lawyers caused or (the last two cases) might have caused. But, you'll recall that I've mediated between two and three thousand lawyers. And out of two thousand lawyers, five bad apples is equivalent to 0.25% of the total who were a barrier to settlement. That's one quarter of one per cent in old money. The rest were really pretty good, and many, probably most, were excellent. I know it's an unfashionable thing to say but I actually think the lawyers I've mediated are for the most part a credit to their profession.

And that means that by the time of the mediation, at least in my experience, most lawyers – the overwhelming majority, in fact – have already advised their clients that their litigation comes with risk attached, and will probably have discussed the level of the risk. And most will tell the mediator as much. Not necessarily first thing in the mediation, no. Nobody has ever greeted me with "Good morning Martin, nice to meet you, and can I say at the outset that I assess the risk of losing this case at 50%". At the start of the mediation they're probably still going to be making the arguments that they've been paid good money to make about how great their client's case is. Which is fair enough. But a bit later on, once trust has been established, they'll normally confide that, yes, there's a degree of risk, and be willing to discuss it.

And if – occasionally – a lawyer is not willing to concede that there's a degree of risk, and if they carry on pronouncing that their client simply

---

6 That was a joke: we don't really put notches on our flip charts. My flip chart is just a bit battered, that's all. Those are scuffs, not notches. I promise.

must succeed there are some simple questions that will enable the mediator to draw out the fact that the litigation nevertheless has an element of risk. The mediator might try asking something along these lines:

"So, you're guaranteeing that your client is going to win then?"

"So, your advice is that this case has no element of risk at all?"

"So, you're saying that this case is 100% certain to succeed?"

Ask any of those questions and even the boldest lawyer will have a momentary vision of their indemnity insurance policy riding towards them brandishing increased insurance premiums and concede that, yes, of course, all litigation carries some degree of risk.

And if the parties don't have lawyers, they will probably still know intuitively that litigation is risky. Indeed, there is often a correlation between the decision not to use lawyers and an awareness of the generally unsatisfactory nature of litigation. The last time I asked "So, you're not using lawyers then?" I got a hollow laugh in response and was informed that all lawyers were "useless, a total waste of space". That was a bit of an open goal for any mediator and the obvious follow-up question about whether that view would extend to the judge trying the case swiftly received the confirmation that, yes, the judge would most likely be useless too. Which sad analysis got us straight to where we needed to be in under two minutes: since the judge was not to be relied upon, the outcome of the case couldn't be relied upon either.

By drawing out what the parties to the dispute already know – or have been advised – about litigation risk the mediator can avoid lecturing them about the risks of litigation in general, or the extent of the risk in a particular case. Lecturing the parties about anything is never a good look for a mediator. It's their case, their negotiation, and their decision on whether to settle. Nothing there for us to lecture them about. Plus, drawing out what the parties already know is many times more powerful than the mediator telling them the same thing, because if it comes from them or their advisors it must be right. But once the confirmation that (like all litigation) the dispute in question carries some degree of risk does come from the parties or their advisors, that gives the mediator permission, as it were, to reframe the litigation as a risk-bearing proposition, and that as we've seen is the key to generating flexibility.

And that's all we mediators need to work with. *Some* degree of risk. *Some* chance that the case might go pear shaped in court. The more bullish individuals, or even (occasionally) the more bullish advisors may try to tell you that their case is so strong and the risk so minimal that they are willing to take that risk. The stuff about how minimal the risk is may be bluster. I think that often it is. People reckon that if they persuade the mediator that they really, really do mean to go to court, then the mediator will communicate that to the other side and they'll get a better deal. And the mediator may have to make a judgement call about whether this is bluster, in which case I'd leave it alone, and concentrate on building trust (because if they are blustering at you, the trust isn't there yet) or a genuine view, in which case it may be worth suggesting that they invest some time going through the factors in Mr Justice Lightman's speech so as to temper the conviction that the risk is insignificant and that a successful outcome is guaranteed.

But the good news is that once a degree of risk is acknowledged it's not normally necessary to get into a discussion about the extent of the degree of risk. The precise quantification of the risk of losing tends to matter less than the fact that there is *some* risk of losing. Let me explain why.

Risk aversion and Loss Aversion

People are generally risk averse.

You don't have to take my word for that. In the 1970s two psychologists, Daniel Kahneman (who was subsequently awarded the Nobel Prize for this work) and Amos Tversky (who wasn't[7]) used the simplest

---

7 Nobody said life was fair. See The First Noble Truth.

imaginable risk to demonstrate risk aversion: the risk that a spun coin will come down tails rather than heads. They found that if they offered people $10 if the coin came down heads, but on the basis that people had to pay $10 if the coin came down tails, the majority of people wouldn't play.

That's not all that they found. It seems that improving the potential gains – in effect building a "risk premium" into the equation – will, at lower magnitudes, make people a little more willing to take the risk. Kahneman and Tversky's work together with subsequent research apparently suggests that the risk premium has to be about twice the potential loss before most people are tempted i.e., if $20 dollars are won if the coin comes down heads, but only $10 dollars lost if it comes down tails, more people may be tempted to "play".

We may put this unwillingness to take risks (until the risk premium reaches a sufficient magnitude, and sometimes not even then) down to loss aversion. For nearly all of us, losses weigh more heavily than gains. Most people would rather hold onto what they have than risk losing what they have in an attempt to win more. You'd be much more upset if you lost £10 than you would be pleased if you found £10. So the potential gain has to be bigger than the potential loss to compensate and tempt people to take a chance. It's been suggested that this loss aversion is the product of our evolution. In a survival-of-the-fittest situation where resources were scarce, losing out on a day's food might have meant death, whereas winning an extra day's food didn't (in the days before deep freezes) mean one could necessarily go for an extra day without food. Is that really the reason? I have no idea, but it sounds plausible enough.

What's more, and I think this is important to the mediator, loss aversion increases with the magnitude of the potential loss. For most people, there comes a point where the magnitude of the loss is such that no risk premium can compensate for the potential loss. That too may be a product of our evolution. If the downside of a risky venture isn't so bad, well then, it might in the survival-of-the-fittest contest have made sense to give it a go, because if it didn't come off, nothing much would have been lost. But if the downside of the risk might be death, then whether success meant an extra day's food, or an extra two day's food, or even wild parties and binge eating for a week, the risk probably wasn't worth taking. Sooner or later, we'd have been unlucky, and the consequences would have been terminal.

You don't have to take Kahneman and Tversky's or anyone else's word for any of this either. I didn't. I've tried a variation of this experiment when teaching my Zen and the Art of Mediation course which I have taught at Norwich's wonderful University of East Anglia (well, some one has to….) as well as to other lawyers or business people, and you can try it too, either as a thought experiment in the comfort of your own mind, or you could do this with a group of colleagues or friends. Some of the other experiments in this book are strictly thought experiments only, but this one you probably could try in the real world without it leading to social embarrassment, legal complications or to your arrest for cruelty to cats. Provided of course that you don't get carried away and actually gamble large sums on the toss of a coin. If you do that, I'm afraid neither my publishers nor I can accept any responsibility.

Anyhow, this is what I've found. If I suggest to a roomful of students that my lecture could do with a bit of spicing up and propose a game of chance where I spin a coin and give a volunteer £0.08 if it comes down heads, but that they have to give me £0.08 if it comes down tails, there's not usually universal interest. You may think that simply says something about my lecturing ability and the interest that generates generally. My lecturing style may be part of the reason for the lack of enthusiasm, certainly. I suspect that part of the reason is also good old British embarrassment, and part of it may be that that they think it's a trick question. Perhaps also at that very low level the sum involved is almost too small to make it worth putting one's hand up and risking embarrassment. But even so, several hands do go up to show willingness to play, and with a bit of cajoling I can usually get around half of them to agree to play the game for a stake of £0.08. By the way, if you're wondering why I used £0.08 and multiples thereof for this experiment and not some other "rounder" figure then, no, it's not an attempt to demonstrate the inherently random nature of the universe. There's a reason. Yes, I have a plan here. But we'll come to that a bit further down the line. If you try this experiment, you don't have to use £0.08 or multiples thereof. You can use any number you like between £0.01 and £0.10 to start with. Be my guest.

Back to my students, if I increase the amount of the gamble by a factor of ten, to £0.80, I probably get about the same number of volunteers. Sometimes a few less, sometimes even a few more. If I get more that may just be because I've finally got their attention, and they've stopped looking at their mobile phones, but it may also be that £0.80 is just a bit more worth playing for than £0.08. I don't know, I haven't seen this suggested, but maybe that's an evolutionary thing too; when the potential gain is too small to make a difference, it makes no sense expending energy on it at all[8].

But if I go up by another factor of ten, to £8.00, I start to lose hands. By which I don't mean that the extremities on the end of my arms drop off: I mean that quite a few of the hands that have been raised around the room to indicate a willingness to gamble are dropped. The days of generous student grants are long gone, if they ever existed, and £8 is a lot of money for most students, and the risk of losing that sum appears to weigh more heavily with quite a few students than the chance to win another £8 does. There may be a few brave souls who are still up for it, but not so many.

Perhaps the difference between those who are still up for it and those who aren't isn't that the former are indeed braver or less loss averse than the latter group: perhaps the "braver" group are just a bit better off (or think that they are) so that they feel they can afford to lose £8.00. My guess, and I have no way of proving this, but it fits with my observations both when lecturing and when mediating, is that *most people won't gamble more than they can afford to lose*. And for quite a few students that point sets in at £8.00. Whereas if I try the same experiment when addressing a room full of lawyers on mediation technique, or perhaps a room full of business people when I've been asked to address them on

---

8 I can feel another Nobel Prize heading my way....

negotiation[9], there are a few more takers at the level of £8.00. Lawyers are not renowned for being risk takers, but they are renowned for being Fat Cats, so I'm guessing that the reason isn't that the lawyers are all devil-may-care gamblers, while the students are all boringly-risk-averse, but that the lawyers have more money and can afford to lose £8, as, presumably, can the businesspeople (if they can't, the economy's in deep trouble, folks).

Back to the students, if I raise the stakes by another order of magnitude, to £80, then I'm pretty much out of volunteers. It would seem that there aren't many students (at least at any institution where I've spoken) who can afford to lose £80 of their precious student loan, or even of the Bank of Mum and Dad's student loan, on the toss of a coin.

The reaction of the lawyers or business people I've spoken to when I raise the stake to £80 is not unlike the reaction of the students at £8. Most of them are out of the game. I've not kept a record of the precise numbers[10] but if anything there's probably less enthusiasm than there was at £8 amongst the students.

Raise the stakes again to £800 and across the board I'm pretty much out of volunteers. A couple of philanthropic lawyers may enquire whether this would be for charity (nope) but generally we're now well above the amount that your average lawyer or business person can afford to lose on the toss of a coin. Up the stake to £8,000 and there's not the slightest interest. Perhaps the lawyers and business people I talk to aren't rich enough. And at £80,000, well, we're well into oligarch territory, because no one who doesn't own at least three yachts and a premiership football club is likely to be able to contemplate losing £80,000 on the toss of coin.

If you go for this experiment yourself, you may find that loss aversion kicks in at a different price point, depending on how well off you, or those you're trying this with, are feeling. But I'm betting that at the

---

9 William Ury was unavailable.

10 Bang goes the Nobel prize.

point where the stake is too much to lose comfortably, you'll find the same thing; loss aversion sets in, and people don't want to take the risk.

You could also try adding in a risk premium. This is best done at the point where people's appetite for risk is very much waning, because that's the point at which a risk premium might tip the scales. In my examples, that point is the £8 stake for the students, and £80 for the lawyers and business people. Doubling the stake, which is about where Kahneman and Tversky found that the risk premium would start to tempt people, means offering the students £16 if they won and only taking £8 off them if they lost. Or, it meant stakes of £+160/-£80 respectively for the lawyers and businesspeople. Obviously, this now becomes a pretty good bet. If a coin were tossed a hundred times, and came down heads precisely fifty times and tails fifty times, and if you collected £16 for each win and paid out £8 for each loss, you'd make a profit of £400. That would become £4,000 at the higher stakes for the lawyers and the business people. Almost worth a lawyer getting out of bed for. And, yes, we're likely to encounter what Kahneman and Tversky and others have found. As the bet gets more attractive, a few hands go up again, attracted by the risk premium. But, here's the thing. Not so many. Not all of them. Yes, it's a good bet now. And played out over one hundred tosses of a coin, the players are almost certain to win handsomely. But, one hundred goes aren't on offer. It's one go, and one go only. And faced with one chance only, people display an instinctive understanding of the First Noble Truth: life is unsatisfactory. The rewards may now be tilted in their favour, but people still focus disproportionately on the loss. And if the stakes are raised to a level where they really can't afford the loss, people are still reluctant, even where there's a risk premium. Sure, the rewards may be greater, but to reap the rewards you have to win first, and you might not, and if you really can't afford the loss, that's a risk you can't afford to run: "It may be a good bet, but it's just my luck that the coin comes down tails...." So if one ups the stakes by one order of magnitude, to £+160/-80 for the students or £+1,600/-800 for the lawyers, there's not many up for the challenge despite the risk premium making it a "good bet" because at that level, they really, really can't afford the loss.

The other variable one can play with is to tweak the chances of winning. One can ask people to imagine that the coin is "bent", in other words that it has a better than even chance of coming down heads, to the extent that their chances of winning are doubled. Even if the stake is reset at the same amount for both winning and losing, this again becomes a good bet. Toss the coin one hundred times, and if it came down heads exactly twice as often as tails[11], and you received £8 for each win but paid out £8 for each loss, you'd make a profit of £266 and some pennies on top. And, once again, at the point where players are starting to drop out, a few more will be tempted to stay with the game. But, once again, not so many. Not all of them. And once again, increase the stakes by one order of magnitude, to £80 for the students, or £800 for the lawyers and the business people, and we'll find that they're mostly out of the game again. Once the stakes have risen beyond the amount people can comfortably contemplate losing, even offering them a coin with a 2:1 chance of winning makes little difference.

Are people more swayed to gamble by a risk premium i.e., a bigger reward for winning, (but carrying the same risk of losing) or by a better chance of winning? Good question. I'm not aware of any research here and I don't think my rather small sample is going to be statistically significant[12]. But for our purposes the key point is this: at or about the point where people really cannot afford to lose, they become risk averse. Loss aversion holds them back. That point – the point where people can no longer afford to lose – may come at different points for different people, determined either by their wealth or by their attitude to wealth. But for almost everyone, there comes a point where the potential losses make the bet unattractive. Offering a risk premium, or tweaking the odds, will encourage some people to stick with the risk a little bit longer (particularly if at the point where the risk premium or the tweaked odds are offered it's a bit marginal for them as to whether they could afford to lose) but the point will nevertheless come where the potential loss is high enough for loss aversion to hold them back.

---

11 Yes, I know. 100 isn't divisible by three, so the coin couldn't come down heads exactly twice as often as tails. Cut me some slack here, ok?

12 Definitely no Nobel prize.

And there you go. The mediator mostly doesn't need to get into an argument with litigants or their advisors about how big the risk of losing is, nor even about how much they might win. That may make a difference to their decision, but only at the margins. Generally, once people are uncomfortable enough with the level of the potential losses, then the precise quantification of the risk tends to matter less than the fact that there is some risk, and people become risk averse at that point. Which means that once the case has been reframed as a risk-bearing proposition, risk aversion should kick in and generate movement towards settlement. Quod erat demonstrandum, as we don't say in Norfolk.

All of which does, however, raise a great big whopping question for the mediator: if people intuitively know that litigation involves risk, and if they're all so risk adverse…..why is anyone litigating at all?

Might there be a class of people who aren't loss averse at all? Well, I don't think I've ever mediated anyone who truly had no loss aversion, though that doesn't mean they might not exist. Perhaps some folk who have what the rest of us would call a gambling addiction in fact don't have loss aversion? I don't know. That's outside my field. But, at any rate, we don't normally see people with a gambling addiction at mediation. And I do believe that just about everyone I've mediated was loss averse.

Which isn't to say that I haven't sometimes seen people in mediation who initially presented as not being loss averse. It's just that once I got to know them, they simply turned out to have a different notion of what would constitute loss from the rest of us. The last case I mediated that didn't settle was a couple of months ago in the West Midlands. It was another of those inheritance disputes that divide sibling from sibling, and in this case two sisters were fighting over an inheritance that neither had really counted on receiving. The Defendant had received the whole of the unexpected bounty from a fairly distant relative, and was seeking to defend it from her sister's claim to a half share. There have probably been warring tribes that wiped each other off the face of the planet in pre-history who nevertheless liked each other more than these two sisters did, but that wasn't ultimately the problem. I've seen cases settle despite similar levels of dislike, precisely because loss aversion kicked in. But as the day went on it became apparent that the Defendant wasn't loss averse *in financial terms*. She lived what one might call an alternative lifestyle, committed very much to healing the world (though not her sister) through the use of crystals. Or perhaps it was the other way round, and the crystals were using her to heal the world? I shouldn't presume. At any rate, hers wasn't an expensive lifestyle. She hadn't expected any inheritance from this relative. She didn't need the money. Nor did the crystals. We looked at the worst outcome (from her point of view) if the case went to court. That would have meant that her sister would get half the estate, and the Defendant might have to pay the legal costs of both sides out of her share. Even then, she would still have been left with more money than she or her crystals were likely to be able to spend over the rest of her days. She rather disapproved of money, actually (though not as much as she disapproved of her sister). And she was either going to be left with (if she lost) more money than she needed or entirely approved of, or (if she won) even more money than she needed or approved of. "Loss", to her, didn't mean losing the money. That didn't even register on her "loss" scale. Loss, to her, meant something else. I'll try to explain this, though I may not have fully grasped the subtleties here, for which I apologise. But I'll do my best. To her, "loss" meant losing the ability to feel the frequency at which the crystals vibrated and – obviously – if she were untrue to herself by "giving" the hateful sister a penny she might lose that crucial ability. It wasn't that she wasn't loss averse; it was just that the loss that she was averse to wasn't losing the money. I tried to explore with her whether the consequence of going to trial could cause bad vibrations that might have a similar adverse effect should the judge rule in favour of the Claimant, but it appeared that this outcome would not cause the same problems. If the judge awarded the money to the Claimant, well and good: the Defendant would still have been true to herself, and the crystals would recognise that. Or perhaps the crystals wouldn't have recognised it, as such, perhaps the point is that the Defendant herself would have known that she hadn't given her sister a penny, at least not voluntarily, and therefore she would still have had the clear conscience that would enable her to resonate on the crystals' frequency. I don't know. I don't do resonating with crystals. Sorry.

Anyway, as a result, there was, and could have been, no deal. Not because the Defendant had no loss aversion, but because the loss of the inheritance that the parties were litigating about just wouldn't have been a "loss" to her. Perhaps a transformative mediator could have done better and got all sides vibrating on the correct frequency? Well, maybe: good luck with that. But, this was a pretty rare case. The circumstances were extreme. I'm not even sure I can think of another quite like it. Mostly, people are loss averse, and tend to see loss in terms of the outcome of the litigation: that's generally why they're fighting the case so hard! And that brings us back to our question: if people are so loss averse, and if that loss aversion makes them risk averse, and if they know (intuitively, or because they're so advised) that the litigation carries risks, just why are they litigating? And that may even be a topical question in the field of cognitive psychology, because I am told that some recent studies on loss aversion have raised what may be a similar conundrum: yes, people are loss averse, as Kahneman and Tversky found, but their actual behaviour – the choices they make – doesn't necessarily seem to reflect that loss aversion as much as Kahneman and Tversky's work would have suggested.

Welcome to my world, you cognitive psychologists[13]. I wouldn't presume to comment on those studies, or to tell you what's going on here in a wider context, because cognitive psychology isn't what I know about. I can't even spell it without the help of a spell checker. But I think I've done enough mediations to be able to offer a guess as to what's going on in a mediation. Here goes. Yes, people are loss averse, at the point where they can't afford to lose. But there's a counter balancing mechanism at work here, which is that we often seem to have a blind spot for the loss, or for the extent of the possible loss, until something or someone makes it seem real. It's almost as if the loss is too horrible to contemplate, so our first instinct is not to look at it too closely. Perhaps this has some evolutionary basis too? Maybe if our ancestors didn't have this initial "loss blind spot", they'd have been so

---

13 I've always wanted to say something like that.

cowed by any risk of any loss that they wouldn't have dared to get out of bed in the morning. They might have refused to go looking for food at all because there might be a lion ten kilometres away. Whereas with this initial blind spot for loss, they'd go looking until something made the lion loom larger, at which point loss aversion and risk aversion would kick in. Perhaps that's the best evolutionary set-up of all? I don't know; as far as this evolutionary survival-of-the-fittest stuff is concerned, I'm making it up as I go along. And it could be that this is all just another way of saying that until there's some degree of risk (for example, from a closer lion) then the loss aversion doesn't matter. And maybe that's right: it's certainly true, as I've said, that in a mediation the mediator needs some degree of risk to work with. But to me as a mediator, it does feel as if people have an initial blind spot about the extent of the possible loss, even if they are aware of a degree of risk, until someone brings the loss into large and scary focus. And that someone would have to be the mediator, folks.

It comes down to this. Until the mediator helps the parties focus on the extent of the possible loss, they may not realise that, actually, they can't afford the loss. And loss aversion won't kick in fully until they've realised that. I guess it's understandable. We all of us prefer not to look too closely at something horrible. I'm still working up the resolve to watch the highlights of Norwich City's last defeat.

It is perhaps easier to give you an example of how this initial blind spot for loss can manifest in a mediation than to try to explain it in theoretical terms. I'm a bit of a stupid bear when it comes to theoretical explanations anyway. And I've been meaning to run you through a mediation from start to finish ever since I started writing this little book. Just as an example of how the process might work. It would be a shame if the only mediation set out in any detail in a book on mediation were one conducted by Humphrey Forbes-Smythe QC. Not so much Zen and the Art of Mediation, more Zen and the Art of Totally Failing to Mediate. So, here's the plan. I'll run you through a mediation and, as we go, we'll look out for that initial blind spot for loss, and see how it affects the outcome of the mediation. Ok?

CHAPTER SIX

A mediation

Now, this isn't based on an actual mediation. Nor is it stitched together from a couple of actual mediations. You know already that confidentiality would prevent me from setting out any of the facts of a real mediation. And as I said I would in the Introduction, when, in the course of this book, I've told you about things that did happen in mediations, in the interests of maintaining confidentiality I've always tweaked sufficient details to protect the anonymity of those involved – clients and lawyers alike – and then mixed and matched things from different mediations so that I'm never writing about one actual mediation. But in this chapter I'm going to run through pretty much a whole mediation with you. Which means that if I were to take a real mediation, any real mediation, or any couple of real mediations, even, and just tweak the details here or there, there would still be a risk that the outline of an actual mediation might remain visible beneath the details that I've tweaked, like the outline of a sunken ship at low tide. So, I've made this one up entirely. But, I promise you, it's typical. In fact, precisely because it's made up, it's almost *more* typical than any real-life mediation could be, because every actual mediation has its own features which make it unique and not (quite) entirely typical. Whereas this one is, well, as typical as I can make it. You can be the mediator.

The dispute is a relatively modest one. The Claimant claims £100,000 for the supply of widgets to the Defendant. Ok, £100,000 is a lot of money to me, and perhaps to you, dear reader, and it is to the parties in this case too, but in the context of the cases that people litigate over, it's not the biggest. And we'll keep it simple: there's no counterclaim. The Defendant company simply denies that they are indebted to the Claimant. They say the widgets were defective, and not fit for purpose.

We'll assume that you have done what Humphrey Forbes-Smythe QC couldn't be bothered to do, and that you have arrived at the mediation venue not just on time, but early. If punctuality is the politeness of princes, then arriving not just on time, but ahead of time, represents the good manners of mediators. More than that, arriving early has a lot of practical advantages for the mediator. It means you can check the mediation rooms to make sure that all is in order, that no one can overhear what's being said in the other party's room, and ideally make sure that there's a flip chart in each room in case you need one later on. If you arrive at the venue before the parties to the dispute that's best of all because you can find out where everything is and then greet them when they arrive, show them to their rooms, and get them coffee. That's good, firstly, because mediation runs on caffeine, and, secondly, because it suggests that the mediator is in control of the proceedings. After all, he must be in control if he knows where each side's rooms are *and* where the coffee is, and that will help to start to establish trust in the mediator. Thirdly, whilst you're showing the parties to their rooms and generally pottering around getting them tea and coffee, you'll be picking up a lot of useful information about each side. Who's nervous? Who's bullish? Who just wants two sugars and lots of milk in their coffee? All important stuff for the mediator to know. And even if the parties get there before you (which is possible – it's kind of a big day for them, so they may want to arrive very early, often to have a discussion with their lawyers ahead of the kick off) the fact that you too have got there early will show the parties that it's a big day for you too, and that you care, which again helps to build trust.

We'll also assume that, unlike Humphrey Forbes-Smythe QC, you dressed to look the part: smart, professional, but unlike him, approachable. I have no doubt whatsoever that Humphrey's beautiful heavily pin striped double breasted suit was the handiwork of one of Saville Row's finest and most expensive tailors, and perhaps it was just me who thought there was something a bit gangster about it. Either way, I'm sure he could have got away with that, but what really ruined Humphrey's look were the dark glasses. Dearie me, as he himself might say. You'll have to trust me on this one, dark shades are not a good look for a mediator. Perhaps that's because, as everyone who has ever watched one of the Terminator films knows, the one essential fashion accessory for killer cyborgs from the future is a pair of dark shades. Or perhaps it's because the eyes are the window to the soul and all that. I don't know. But I do know this: dark glasses make it harder to establish a connection. Ok, I know, Humphrey could have had an eye condition. He could have. Possibly. And, yes, there certainly are mediators who have an eye condition who may need or who may prefer to wear dark glasses for medical reasons. And, yes, they should be allowed to mediate too. I mean that. Sincerely. Reader, I am one such mediator. I have an eye condition. It's not a big deal, but I wear dark shades much of the time when I'm not mediating, not because I want to look like a killer cyborg from the future, but because they help my eyes. That's why I *know* that dark glasses don't help when you're mediating. I'm lucky enough to be able to go without them in mediations, mostly. But sometimes, I do need them, and the moment I put them on I sense how the tint can operate as a barrier. So if I get the feeling that I might need to put them on, I take a moment to explain to the parties why I'm putting them on, and make a little bit of a joke about it not being a good look for a mediator. And people are very kind, and smile, and it's fine. But just to walk in wearing a dark suit and dark shades without a word of explanation wasn't great.

So, your appearance and your early arrival have made a good impression. Trust is starting to build before the mediation has even started. That's good. You're already ahead of Humphrey Forbes-Smythe QC (not that we're setting the bar very high, there). You probably found that the parties weren't ready to talk to you immediately, because they needed to run through stuff with their lawyers. That's cool. It's their day. If they need some time alone, you're fine with that. But you explain that once they're ready for you, you'd like to have a brief preliminary chat with each side on their own, just to chat over how the day is going to work, and to see if they have any questions. And you ask them how long they'd like to talk amongst themselves before you can join them for that chat, and then agree a time when you'll come back, all of which sets an altogether more relaxed tone than Humphrey Forbes-Smythe QC coming into the room and pretty much opening with "Ready for the plenary, Molly?" Oh, and you've read the papers, and you actually know the parties' names. You're streets ahead of Humphrey, now.

Then, when the parties are ready for you, you have a brief chat with each of them about the ground rules for the mediation. The Mediation Police says that one of the mediator's first jobs at a mediation is to make sure that the parties understand those ground rules (as to confidentiality and so on). And, yes, that's important. If the Mediation Police says it is, then it must be. Who am I to argue with the Mediation Police? Yes, ok, first in line, normally, but they're right on this occasion: this stuff is important. But what I think is more important about that opening chat with each side is that it maintains the relaxed tone you've set and is a nice, gentle, relaxed way to get to know them a bit and to ease them into the mediation. Marching in and kicking off with "Ready for the plenary, Molly?", even if everyone present knew what a plenary session was, and even if Molly were the correct name, is still the mediation equivalent of pushing a nervous swimmer straight into icy water. And whilst some folk get over the shock of being pushed into icy water and pronounce that it's "lovely once you're in", there are others who leap straight back out and who run home screaming, and that's not really the start to a mediation that we're looking for. What's more, a "Ready for the plenary, Molly?" start is going to lead to a whole lot of adrenalin flowing through everyone's systems. And we don't want adrenalin in a mediation. Adrenalin is the "fight or flight" hormone, and we're not looking for either of those, thank you very much. And it takes an hour for adrenalin to clear out of the bloodstream, so if we start by triggering a massive discharge of adrenalin we can write off the next hour anyway. Whereas a gentle opening, with time for questions, enables the parties to feel at ease and in control.

And on the subject of letting the parties feel in control, you take the opportunity to ask them, during that opening chat, whether they'd like a joint session. Ok: if you're a Disciple of the Sacred Joint Session, I'm just going to have to ask you to be strong and bear with me here. Have faith. It's going to be alright. There won't be retribution from on high if they don't want a joint session. The Mediation Police won't storm the mediation and declare it null and void on the grounds that it's "not a proper mediation". I promise. You can trust me on this[1]. Breathe

---

1 I'm making this mediation up, remember, so I should know.

deeply, and if you're at home, and not going to be driving any time soon, pour yourself a stiff drink. You can tell your significant other that I said you needed it. Alright now? Ok then, back to our mediation, and guess what: neither side wants a joint session. Just like they mostly don't, if asked. Which is good, because avoiding a joint session keeps the adrenalin from flowing, and saves us spending half an hour or more hurling moral or legal certainties that just serve to entrench everyone's positions at each other, and means you can get straight on with talking to the parties in private sessions.

First, let's meet the Claimant. He's the owner of small family widget making company. He built the company up from nothing. He's proud of his company. He's on the board of the National Institute of Widget Makers (West Midlands Region). He's proud of that, too. It's one of the first things he tells you. And he's cross – outraged even – at the slur that his widgets were not fit for purpose. He's been making these widgets for thirty years, and every widget that leaves his factory carries his personal stamp of quality. Not literally, you understand, that would actually impair the performance of the widgets, but metaphorically. But, he's also a reasonable man. He tells you that too. He doesn't really want to go to trial. He could do without the legal costs, for a start. He's advised that by the end of the trial his costs could be £50,000 on top of what he's already spent and that even if successful he might only recover 60% of those costs[2]. He can't really understand how the costs could be that high but he certainly doesn't want to be incurring any more. He's already incurred £5,000 in legal fees, which adds to his general dissatisfaction with the whole situation. And he could do without the waste of his time. His time is important. He has important things to do. Things he'd rather be doing. He's on the Board of the National Institute of Widget Makers (West Midlands Region), did he mention that? In truth, he's a mild man who, though angry, doesn't really want the confrontation, hasn't really got the stomach for the legal costs involved, and he's probably finding the whole thing a bit stressful, though he doesn't actually say the last bit to you. What he does tell you is that as a result of all of this, he's come to the mediation to do a deal, and he's willing

---

2 For any non-lawyers, there's usually a proportion of the legal costs in any case that aren't recoverable from the opposition, even after winning in court.

to be reasonable. More than reasonable, in fact. He's willing to be generous, there's no other word for it. There's a limit beyond which he won't be pushed, because he's pretty angry, and – what's more – he's in the *right*, but the bottom line is that he wants to do a deal, and as a result, he tells you that the Defendant has an opportunity to get away lightly today.

Now let's meet the Defendant. Or rather, since the Defendant is a limited company, let's meet the Defendant's Managing Director. To speak plainly, and he always speaks plainly, it's just how he is, no offence, but he doesn't really have time for this nonsense. The Defendant company is a successful business and employs over one hundred people. Unlike the Claimant, he might add, who's always going on about being on the Board of some trade association no one's ever heard of in order to try to disguise the fact that he's a glorified one-man band. But, look here, the MD is a commercial man. He'll always tell it like it is. If he was liable, he'd pay. End of story. But the truth is, he's not liable. The Claimant bit off more than he could chew with this order. This job was too big for him. So, the Defendant isn't liable. End of story. And he's got an expert's report that says the Claimant's widgets were defective. From a board member of the Royal Society of Chartered Widget Makers! Ha! End. Of. Story. Like the Claimant, his costs of fighting this would be £50,000, which he understands. He's litigated before, you know. He's a commercial man, and sometimes that means having to litigate. To speak plainly, it comes with the territory. And as a result he understands that he'd only recover about 60% even if he wins. He's already spent £5,000 on the legal costs of this ridiculous claim, and by rights he should have those back as part of any settlement. Worse still, the whole thing is taking up his time, and his business needs him. Time is money!

As you chat with the parties, you listen, attentively, nodding to show your understanding and prompting them gently to go on when necessary. You know much of what they're telling you, of course, because you've read the case papers. Unlike Humphrey Forbes-Smythe QC. He hadn't even opened the envelope the case papers were wrapped in. And in fairness to Humphrey, most mediators will tell you that they always get sent far too many papers. I think that the lawyers preparing the papers for a mediation sometimes forget that the mediation isn't a trial, and that the mediator isn't a judge. Unlike a judge, a mediator isn't concerned to evaluate the evidence. So, mediators simply don't need as much documentation. In fact, there's a school of thought in mediation circles that says the bigger the bundle of documents supplied to the mediator, the lower the chances of a successful settlement. For that reason some mediators, particularly a number who are established and successful, think it's legitimate not to read what they have been sent.

That's not my view. No, I don't need to – and shouldn't try to – evaluate the evidence. And if any solicitor who instructs me as a mediator is reading this then, firstly, thanks very much for buying the book and, secondly, if you could have a think about reducing the volume of papers you send to me next time, that would be great. Not because it would save me time – though it would – but precisely because part of my job as your mediator is to avoid getting sucked into the detail to the point where I start to form a view of my own, because that makes me a less effective mediator. But, I promise you this: what you do send to me, I will read. I will read it because you thought it was important enough to copy and send to me, so that makes it important enough for me to read. And if you, dear reader, are a mediator, I think you should do the same. Humphrey Forbes-Smythe QC may have said that he didn't need to read the papers to enable him to settle Mary's case, but in saying that he just demonstrated how little he understood the mediation process. As a mediator, you don't read the background papers so that *you* can settle the case. It wasn't your case to settle, actually, Humphrey. It belonged to Mary and to the Bank, and every dispute you ever mediate belongs not to you, dear fellow mediator, but to the parties and they will settle it themselves, given a bit of help. You read the papers so that you are able to understand and affirm the parties' positions, that's all. "Understanding is the heartwood of well-spoken words" said the Buddha. The First Noble Truth tells us that the parties to a dispute are dissatisfied at being in dispute, and as we've seen, as a result what they need first is understanding and affirmation. Holding oneself out as altogether too lofty to need to trouble oneself with the details of someone else's life is the very opposite of offering them understanding and affirmation. It smacks of contempt. That's why Mary started to cry when Humphrey said he hadn't read the papers.

In fact, a mediator or dispute resolver in my view needs to do *more* than simply reading the papers. On its own, that isn't enough. You also need to be able to *demonstrate* that you understand the background. I once met a well known mediator who told me that he doesn't bother to read what he's sent, he just gets a pack of those sticky yellow post-it notes and covers the papers he has been sent with post it notes, which makes it look as if he has read the papers. Now, don't get me wrong. I'm not recommending that. It's dishonest, for a start, and if the parties get the slightest whiff that they can't trust their mediator then the mediation is doomed anyway. But, he had a point. Since as mediators we are offering affirmation, the trick – as he had realised – is not so much to have read and understood the papers as to be *seen* to have read and understood them.

So, yes, I read what I'm sent, and you've read what you were sent for this mediation. I highlight the bits that seem to me important with one of those nifty highlighter pens that put a luminous colour on the paper and also on my hands. Doing that is good (a) because it helps me find key bits again during the mediation, and (b) it also demonstrates to the parties, who notice that kind of thing, that I've read the papers[3]. More importantly though, where I can I memorise the locations of key sections in the bundle so that I can demonstrate my familiarity with the substance of the warring parties' positions to them. And you've done the same in this mediation.

---

3 And if you're a mediator who prefers to receive the case papers electronically in order to read them on your computer or tablet you can still do this, since most of these will now allow you to highlight the documents electronically with a special pencil or stylus – and there's a lot to be said for reading the documents electronically, both in terms of saving the planet by printing less, and saving your back by having to carry less, plus, of course you won't get highlighter pen all over your hands.

Imagine, if you will, that we've got through the early stages of the mediation. The Claimant as we've seen is angry, stressed, and generally wound up about the litigation. There's the First Noble Truth. You've empathised. Not to the extent of agreeing that the widgets were perfect, obviously. That's not the mediator's place to decide. But it's obvious that this dispute is time consuming, expensive, and frustrating, that he needs it like the proverbial hole in the head, and that anyone who is on the Board of the National Institute of Widget Makers (West Midlands Region) must have better things to do with their time. You get that. You've demonstrated empathy there, and in so doing, built trust.

You've reached a similar position with the Defendant. The First Noble Truth holds good: despite being a commercial man for whom litigation like this is just an unimportant distraction from grander commercial projects, no offence, he's actually pretty wound up about the dispute too, if only because this tiresome claim from a glorified one-man band is getting in the way of those grander commercial projects. You get that, too, and you've demonstrated empathy there. In so doing, you've built trust in his room also.

Having offered affirmation and demonstrated an understanding of each party's case, and empathised where you can, and thereby established trust, you've tentatively started to reframe the dispute in each room, no longer in terms of the value-judgement-laden stories that the parties have been telling themselves about the dispute – the *quality* (or otherwise) of the widgets, the *soundness* of each side's legal position, the *reasonableness* of their respective actions – but instead framing the dispute as a risk-bearing proposition. And it turns out that you're pushing on a bit of an open door with the Claimant. He's advised by his solicitor that his chances of success are 60 to 70%. Whilst that's pretty good, he can see that this means there's still a significant chance of the litigation going wrong. In truth, it's probably a higher chance than he's comfortable with. At a 30% to 40% downside, it's actually quite a significant risk for a smallish company not used to litigating.

The position is not that dissimilar in the Defendant's room. He's advised that his chances of success are high, 70 to 80%. He acknowledges, however, that this means there's still an element of risk and, whilst – obviously! – it's a small element, being MD of the company, his job is to control risk. He's a commercial man, and commercial men don't like risk when it comes to running a business. End of story.

So, neither side really wants the litigation, both are prepared to reframe the dispute as a risk bearing proposition and both acknowledge that there's an element of risk. And an element of risk is all a mediator needs to work with. What's more, although you're mediating a fight between a case that is likely to win and another case that is even more likely to win[4], there's risk aversion there too; neither is really keen on the risk. So, after a morning spent offering affirmation, empathising and building trust, and then reframing the dispute with the help of the parties' lawyers in terms of risk, after lunch you conclude that the stars are aligned and that it's time to get the parties to put some offers on the table. Over lunch, or just after lunch, can be a good time to do this, by the way, because about fifteen minutes after people have ingested the carbohydrates provided, their blood glucose levels will start to rise, and they'll feel a little bit more positive about things generally and be a bit more likely to make a sensible offer. It's much harder to get a realistic offer out of people who are hungry, and whose blood glucose levels are falling. That's one reason (among many) why it's rarely a good idea for the mediator to rush to getting first offers out before lunch, even if the parties assure you that they're "ready to negotiate".

How low do you think our reasonable, settlement-minded Claimant will go on his claim for £100,000? Well, he starts with a proposal to accept £80,000. He's advised that his chances of success are 60 to 70%; a 70% chance of success equates to a settlement at 70% of the total claim, right? How reasonable is that? That would be £70,000, but he has to start a bit higher, at £80,000, because he knows that there's going to be some haggling, and he needs to leave himself a bit of wiggle room. The Defendant's MD is a bully, he tells you, and is going to want to be seen to knock the Claimant down a bit, so he needs that £10,000 in hand. And he wants his £5,000 legal costs paying. Obviously. If the other side hadn't defended his totally reasonable claim, he wouldn't

---

4 It was ever thus.

have incurred them. So, it's only right that they have to pick those up. He's not backing down on that. So, in total, he wants £85,000.

You may think that an offer of £85,000, out of a claim for £100,000 plus costs doesn't sound so reasonable. But don't worry. Actually, the Claimant knows it won't settle at that level. This is a first offer. He's putting down a marker, that's all. If you'll permit me a brief digression, at Mediator School they teach you that a Mediation breaks down into distinct phases. Different Mediation Schools call these phases by different names, but they're pretty much the same thing. These phases include the Exploration Phase (finding out what the claim is all about, building trust and exploring the parties' positions) followed by the Negotiation Phase (where the parties exchange offers). Me, I'd probably want to talk about an Opening Phase, or maybe a Building Trust Phase, then a Reframing Phrase, which is then followed by a Negotiating Phase. Anyhow, like so much of what is taught at Mediator School, this idea of phases is both true and not true. True in the very general sense that, yes, there is a part of the mediation where we're exploring each side's position, where we're affirming and (I'd say) empathising and building trust, maybe there's a reframing phase where we're starting to reframe the dispute in terms of risk, and, yes, unless it's a really seriously unsuccessful mediation, there's a part of the mediation where we're exchanging offers. And, yes, the former phase or phases come before the latter. But it's not so true in the sense that the phases aren't distinct and separate. They kind of melt into one another. In the Exploration Phase the parties are telling you just how annoyed they are, and how great their legal positions are. You might call it posturing. And I sometimes think that the first offer is sort of a transitional stage between the posturing and the Negotiating Phase. Yes, it's an offer, but no one thinks for a moment that it's going to be accepted. In that sense, it's not a serious proposal to end the dispute. It's a bit of a hybrid between adopting a posture and making an offer: "Look here: I think my case is so strong that I seriously think £85,000 is a sensible figure to offer! Take that, Defendant!"

The Claimant's first offer very much falls into that category. One more demonstration of how strongly he feels before we get down to the serious business of compromising the claim. He'll go lower. But before he does, he needs to get this last piece of posturing off his chest. You take a moment to consider whether the "offer" is pitched so high that it might derail the negotiation before it's really got going: there are times where it's right for the mediator to talk through with one side or the other whether a particular offer is actually going to be so counterproductive that they might want to re-evaluate whether they really want the mediator to convey it to the other side. But in this case you think that the fall out can be managed, and you decide to convey the offer to the Defendant.

The Defendant's MD greets the offer with peels of laughter. It appears to be the funniest thing he's heard in a long time. And it just proves what he's said all along. The guy just isn't commercial! He hasn't a clue! The MD knew this mediation was a waste of time, and he starts to pack his briefcase, still chortling, since, clearly, we're all wasting our time. End of story!

That's all fine. Many litigants seem to believe that it's obligatory in mediation either to (a) laugh wildly at the other side's first offer, or (b) to make as if to pack up and go home upon hearing it. This time, you've got both responses for the price of one, that's all. What they both signify is that the MD is not settling at that level, and he wants everyone to know it. Which everyone does, actually, even the Claimant. So, you can safely empathise. Yes, first offers can be unrealistic, can't they? The thing is, if this mediation is to work, you tell the MD, we have to get beyond the unrealistic positions and into a *commercial* negotiation. If £85,000 isn't commercial – and you can see from the MD's reaction that it isn't going to fly – then perhaps he'd like to make a commercial offer? After all, he's a commercial man.

Well, yes, he is, and, yes, he would like to make an offer, as it turns out. The briefcase gets unpacked again. His starting point is that the Claimant's claim is hopeless. By rights, the Claimant should pay the Defendant's legal costs of dealing with it. But, yes, he's a commercial man. He hasn't got the time to be dealing with a one-man band and his hopeless case, and he's come to be commercial. And so he responds to the Claimant's first offer to accept £85,000 with a counter-offer that he'll bear his own costs. He wants you to show the Claimant the report from the expert from the Royal Society of Widget Makers, which he's been "keeping up his sleeve" until now and helpfully suggests that you might mention to the Claimant that this report is from a "proper" expert, not some jumped up member of an association of one-man bands, which helpful suggestion you sagely promise to keep up your sleeve for now. Nevertheless, the Defendant anticipates that when the Claimant sees that his claim has nowhere to go he'll be mighty relieved to get out without a costs penalty.

So, £85,000 on the one hand is set against a counter-offer of £0. Not so great. There again, we now have a settlement gap, and it is at least down from £100,000+ (including costs) to £85,000: the negotiation is under way!

The Defendant's offer to bear his own costs goes down like a lead balloon with the Claimant. As does the report from the expert witness from the Royal Society of Widget Makers. It transpires that in the Claimant's eyes that august body consists of a bunch of London based toffs who've mostly never seen a real widget in their lives. If anything, the report just makes the Claimant more determined to fight. And as he ruefully observes, maybe he's going to have to fight after all. Do you think the Defendant has any intention of negotiating a reasonable deal, he asks? You empathise. It doesn't look as if he's getting a deal at £85,000. Was he expecting the Defendant to agree to pay that figure, you ask? No, he tells you, of course he wasn't: it was designed to be a "first shot in the negotiation", that was all. You think out loud as to whether the Defendant's response was the same thing: a first shot, not for one moment put forward with any expectation that it might be expected. Perhaps the level of the Claimant's own first offer pitched right at one end of the spectrum produced a counter-offer at the other end of the spectrum from the Defendant, almost in retaliation? An offer with a subtext that said: "I can make offers that I know won't be accepted every bit as well as you can"? Perhaps the time has come to make an offer that the Claimant thinks might actually be accepted?

The Claimant thinks it has.

He drops to £60,000. Plus his costs, obviously. So, £65,000. He's in full negotiating mode, now. He's advised that he has a 60 to 70% chance of winning so, he tells you, he really ought to be offering £70,000 first, or maybe splitting the difference between the two percentages at 65%. But as he said earlier, he wants to do a deal, and he'll give the Defendant the benefit of the doubt. His chances are 60 to 70%, but he'll take 60% of the claim. Bargain! Plus his costs, obviously. He finds his own reasonableness really quite hard to believe. But this is a more serious offer, the valuation he actually puts on the claim.

If you'll permit me another brief diversion, the negotiating pattern we're seeing from the Claimant here is actually quite typical. When I was at Mediator School I was taught about something called The Three Offer Rule. This Rule, so they said, is derived from research carried out in the United States into the offers made in hundreds or even thousands of mediations. Quite how anyone can research the offers made in a mediation, given that mediations are strictly confidential, I'm not sure. Maybe the mediation rooms were bugged. Mediationgate! You may be sceptical about the proposition that offers follow a particular rule, and I'll admit that I was pretty sceptical when I was first taught about it. In fact, I thought it sounded like what folk in Norfolk would call a load of old squit[5]. But, I can tell you that based on the one thousand plus cases that I've mediated there's something to the Three Offer Rule. So long as you don't interpret it too literally, and view it less as a rule that's always followed (there's no such thing in mediation) and more as a pattern that can be observed (to a greater or lesser extent) in a surprising proportion of mediations, then, I promise you, there's something there.

The Three Offer Rule says that in a negotiation, and specifically in a mediation, the parties often make three offers. The first offer, says the Rule, is a negotiating posture, advanced tactically by the party that proposes it. It's intended to put down a "marker in the sand"[6], but no one seriously expects it to result in a settlement at that figure.

---

5 Hogwash

6 What's the sand doing in the mediation rooms? I don't know either.

The second offer is the party in question's "real" figure. What they think the dispute is worth, in the light of their own (or their lawyer's) risk assessment. The figure they'd be happy, or at least content, to settle at. And the third offer is the price that they'll pay for a settlement, over and above their "real" figure, because whilst they wouldn't be happy to pay or receive that amount, they want certainty, because they want the dispute out of their lives, and because they want to be able to move on and spend their time and money on something other than lawyers [7], and because all these things have a financial value to them.

Now, the Three Offer Rule isn't an iron rule. No one is saying that everyone, or even anyone, *has* to make three offers, and only three offers. You'll come across people who make more, or less. Actually, I'd say that the Three Offer Rule, if interpreted loosely and flexibly, fits comfortable with people making more than three offers. In fact, the parties to a dispute will sometimes make more than one offer at each of the three stages, most often at the second or third stage (less often at the first stage.) For example, our Claimant could easily have followed his initial £85,000 offer with a second offer at £70,000 plus costs (reflecting the upper end of the 60 to 70% range he's been given by his solicitor for his chances of success) before moving on to a third offer at £60,000 plus costs (being the lower end of that 60 to 70% success range). And if he'd done that, I'd have viewed both those his second and third offers as falling within the second stage of the Three Offer Rule. Both would be what he views as a realistic valuation of his claim, based on his legal advice, and, yes, if he'd made those two offers at the second stage he'd have probably have made at least one third stage offer, and therefore ended up making more than three offers over all. I'd say that would still fall within a flexible interpretation of the Three Offer Rule. I did toy with not referring to the rule as the Three Offer Rule at all, but instead calling it the Three-Offer-Rule-which-isn't-a-rule-really-but-more-of-a-general-pattern-and-which-actually-allows-for-the-possibility-of-a-different-number-of-offers-than-three-being-made but my Editor says that "Three Offer Rule" sounds altogether more succinct and memorable. There's 'nowt so queer as folk, hey?

---

7 I know. Strange, isn't it?

I'll share something else I've noticed about the Three Offer Rule with you too, a sort of tweak that we could add to the Rule. We'll call it the Three Offer Rule (Extended Version). This bit isn't from the US researchers in Mediationgate, this bit is me, based on my own experience, so you can give it either more or less weight accordingly. It's your book, so your choice. Now, here's the thing: *the jumps between the stages never get bigger*. By which I mean this: a party to a dispute will rarely move *more* between stages two and three than they did between stages one and two. So, if our Claimant started with a stage one offer to accept £85,000, including costs, an offer not expected to lead to a settlement but made tactically, and then moved to a stage two offer with his real valuation of the case at £65,000, which represents a move of £20,000, the Three Offer Rule (Extended Version) would predict that he won't be offering to reduce his expectations by *more* than £20,000 when it comes to the third stage. In other words, he's not going to be offering to accept less than £45,000 to settle, thank you very much. Now, I'm not saying he necessarily will go that low. The jumps between the stages often get smaller. He might only offer to accept £50,000, or £55,000. But the jumps don't get bigger. And this bit – the bit about the jumps not getting bigger – this bit is almost a hard and fast rule. In all the cases that I've mediated, I'm struggling to think of more than two cases where the jumps got bigger[8]. Nobody – well, almost nobody – negotiates by saying "My claim is worth £100,000 but I'll take £85,000, ok, that wasn't realistic, the value I really put on this case is £65,000, oh, alright then, if it won't settle at that the lowest price I'll accept for settlement is £20,000". The jumps just don't get larger. Remember, though, it's the Three *Offer* Rule. In our mediation the Rule predicts that our Claimant won't be *offering* less than £45,000 but that doesn't mean he might not *accept* something lower but close to that if it were offered by the other side, or maybe floated by the mediator.

Ok? We should get back to our mediation. You've discerned the Three Offer Rule in the Claimant's negotiating pattern, and after an (over) optimistic "marker in the sand" by way of first offer, his second offer to

---

8 This was true when I wrote it. Yesterday, the very next mediation, a jump of £50,000 was followed by one of £150,000. I think the universe is laughing at me. But ok, big deal: so it's three times in over a thousand mediations. It's still rare.

accept £60,000 plus £5,000 for his legal costs represented his genuine valuation of his claim. It's even at the lower end of the range or risk that his lawyer has given him. He thinks the Defendant ought to accept it.

But, no. On the plus side, the Defendant doesn't find the £65,000 offer quite so funny. There's a bit of quiet chortling, and much head shaking, but not the full on hysterics of the response to the earlier offer. And the briefcase remains unpacked, which is also a good sign. On the minus side, that isn't going to be anything like acceptable. Look, he says, the Claimant still isn't in the commercial world. He'll try to make it simple so that the guy can grasp it. The. Claimant. Has. To. Be. Commercial. End of story. But, luckily for the negotiation, it transpires that the Defendant himself is going to be commercial. Just as the Claimant never expected £85,000 to be accepted, but was putting down a marker in the sand, so it transpires that the Defendant never expected the Claimant to go away with nothing. He knows that's not how negotiations work. Both sides have to get something. He gets that. That's commercial. And the fact is that he needs this nonsense off his desk. And, being commercial about it, the brutal commercial truth (did he mention that he's a commercial man?) is that he's going to end up £20,000 out of pocket in respect of his own unrecoverable costs, even after winning the case. So, he'll offer the Claimant £20,000 to buy off his hopeless claim. Just to free up his time. And, he'll bear his own costs. How commercial is that? He's almost surprised at his own commerciality, but nevertheless sends you back to the Claimant with an offer of £20,000. And the settlement gap is down to £45,000.

Pausing for a moment, once again we can see the pattern of the Three Offer Rule. The Defendant's MD really puts very little store by the Claimant's claim: he thinks his expert's report is pretty much the answer to it. Nevertheless, he didn't expect the Claimant to go away with nothing. He knows that wasn't realistic. His first offer was indeed a "marker", made tactically in response to the Claimant's equally tactical first offer. But, the MD knows that the Defendant is going to be £20,000 out of pocket in legal costs even after a successful defence, so he's content to pay that. That's the value he puts on the claim: not a lot, frankly, save for the costs he'll be out of pocket by at the end.

Nuisance Value, if you like. We can also predict, now, that this mediation is going to be touch and go: the Three Offer Rule (Extended Version) suggests that the Claimant won't offer less than £45,000 (that would be another jump of £20,000), whilst we can see that the Defendant has moved £20,000 and we can therefore postulate that he may not offer more than another £20,000 i.e., £40,000 in total. That would leave us £5,000 apart £45,000 against £40,000 and, yes, if we were £5,000 apart there might just be a figure in between the final offers that the mediator could float that would be acceptable to both. But, that's all dependent on each party moving as much again as they've already moved. The Three Offer Rule (Extended Version) doesn't predict that they necessarily will move that much; only that they won't go further So, although on the face of it the settlement gap is down to £45,000 we can see from the underlying pattern of offers that it's going to be close.

You take the offer of £20,000 from the Defendant back to the Claimant.

The Claimant is disappointed. Deflated even. £85,000 may have been a posture, but he had hoped for a deal at £65,000 or thereabouts. That was in line with his legal advice as to his chances of winning, and what could be more reasonable than that? He sighs. You empathise. It's a shame, but sometimes mediations don't settle on the terms of one's own legal advice. As you can see that it's going to be touch and go as to whether this settles, you don't rush to ask the Claimant for another offer, but instead take a few minutes to try another way to reframe the case. You've already reframed it as a risk bearing proposition, and that's helped to generate movement, but now you try reframing it in terms of the consequences of the possible outcomes. Fighting on is going to mean the litigation hangs over him and his business for the next twelve to eighteen months: settling gives him certainty. Certainty now. Today. And, yes, he'd like some of that. In fact, he confides in you, he could do with upgrading his main widget making machine (not that there's anything wrong with the widgets it makes, you understand) but with this litigation hanging over the business, he's had to put that investment on hold. And then, fighting on is going to take up a lot of his time and energy over the next twelve to eighteen months. Whereas a deal today would leave him free to apply his time and energy where he wants to apply it. And yes, he could do with the time. His voice drops almost to a whisper, because this is super confidential, but there's a chance that he might just be about to be elected the Chairman of the National Association of Widget Makers (West Midlands Region) and he'd need as much time as possible in order to discharge the duties of this prestigious post in a manner befitting its importance.

Again, reframing the case in terms other than the legal and moral value judgements that it's been put in so far unlocks a little more movement. He does want to settle and, yes he can go a bit lower. In fact, he'll share his bottom line with you. As low as he's prepared to go. He'll take 50%. If that's not a reasonable offer, what is? It's less than he's advised the claim is worth. Less than his chance of success. But he'll meet the other guy in the middle, not that he deserves it. The good old British compromise. Nobody wins. He'd barely cover the cost of making the widgets in the first place. But never mind. He wants a deal. For all the reasons we've discussed. And for that he'll meet the other guy in the middle and even shake his hand. No lower, mind. That would be to let the other guy win. And that's just not on. No, Sir. Not when he has the stronger case. But, he's come to the mediation to be reasonable, and reasonable he will be. £50,000, half the claim, will do it. Against his better judgement. Despite his better case. Plus his costs, obviously. £55,000 all in. That's his final offer. Lower than that he won't go.

So, it's £55,000 against £20,000. The settlement gap is £35,000. It's getting less, but the Three Offer Rule (Extended Version) tells you that the chances of settlement may be diminishing. The Claimant says £55,000 is his final offer. People often say that something is their final offer, and then make another offer, of course. You're alive to that possibility. But you think this might just be his final offer. We've got beyond most of the value judgements that have defined the case thus far, but there's something basic, something almost primitive about not wanting to go below half, about "not letting the other guy win" that we haven't got beyond. That may well point to this being his last offer. And the Three Offer Rule (Extended Version) predicts that the most the Defendant will do is to add another £20,000, which would take him to £40,000. That would be £15,000 adrift. You know, though, that even if final *offers* are a little way apart, there's still the possibility that the parties will *accept* a figure that lies a little beyond their final offer, so there's still hope for the settlement process.

You take the Claimant's offer to the Defendant, and explain (as you've been asked to) that the Claimant says it's his final offer. This time, the Defendant doesn't find the offer so amusing. The Claimant has moved, he acknowledges that. But it's not enough. He's not going to £50,000, he'll tell you that right away. Let alone £50,000 plus costs. There are no circumstances in which he's meeting this hopeless claim "in the middle", thank you very much. That would be to imply some kind of equivalence between the position of a proper company that has an expert's report condemning the widgets in question from the Royal Institute of Chartered Widget Makers, on the one hand, and a one-man band without a shred of evidence to support his claims on the other. No way will he meet him halfway. That wouldn't be commercial. There's what he calls a "buggeration factor" to this claim, that's all. He'll up his offer to £30,000 but that's it. Not a penny more. Final offer. Frankly, that's £30,000 for nothing and the Claimant would bite his hand off if he were a commercial man. End of story.

You convey the offer of £30,000 to the Claimant, and explain that it's said to be a final offer. The Claimant shakes his head. His disappointment is tangible. You feel that he wants a deal. But he's advised that his chances of success in a £100,000 claim are at least 60%: he can't accept £30,000. It's too low.

Is that it, then? Two final offers: £55,000 against £30,000.

Well, it might be the end of the mediation. End of story, so to speak. If those positions really are final, then we've come up £25,000 short of a deal. Close, but no cigar. Except that they might not be final positions. Time and time again the mediator sees that saying something is a party's final offer doesn't preclude the possibility that they might nevertheless accept something else, ideally something pretty close, if the other side were to offer it or the mediator floats it. As the mediator you wouldn't give up without testing whether these really are final positions. And you have a mediator's hunch[9] that there might be a bit more movement to come. You're pretty sure that if you were able to offer £50,000 the Claimant would swallow his costs rather than go to court over £5,000 worth of costs. You think there's also a pretty good chance that he might even go lower, and would take £45,000. The Three Offer Rule (Extended Version) predicted that he wouldn't go lower than that but left open the possibility that he might go that far. Would he go all the way to the midpoint between the two final offers and accept £42,500? Well, it's some way below 50%, and the 50% marker seemed to matter to him, but the idea of "splitting the difference" could appeal to a man who talked about good old British compromises. Your instinct is that the Claimant really doesn't want to litigate, and might just go for £42,500 but that the figure would probably have to come from the other side, or maybe, just maybe, be floated by you. The Claimant isn't going to offer it.

As for the Defendant, you're less confident. He seems less apprehensive about the litigation. But if £42,500 would do it and get the nuisance off his desk, would he really, really walk away from the settlement and incur £50,000 of litigation costs, not to mention wasting so much of his valuable time, to save another £12,500? Or would he think that uncommercial? There's a chance, at least. Once again, the figure would have to come from the Claimant or be floated by you, he isn't going to offer it.

And float the figure is probably what you'll do. You'll propose the figure of £42,500 in each room, using the "Double Blind" technique. The way this technique works is simple. The Mediator floats a figure. In both rooms. The same figure, obviously. It doesn't work if you use different figures[10]. The figure doesn't have to be the midpoint between final offers, if there's some compelling reason for another figure being the one that's most likely to work, but the midpoint is often the best bet, and it is today. You don't float the figure on the basis that the other side have offered it – they haven't – but on the basis that the parties are

---

9 Other hunches are available.

10 D'oh!

close, that it might be thought a shame (uncommercial even) to incur combined costs of £100,000 when they are £25,000 apart, and that the midpoint between the closing offers is £42,500 – if you could get the other side to that midpoint, you'll ask each side, would they go there? One advantage of this technique is that it's a way of getting the parties to move without them having to make another offer, which they've said they won't do. They're just saying that if the other side came to a particular point, they'd go there too.

And they might just both do it. It would make a lot of sense. Many a mediation has settled on that basis, the parties enticed to make one more move beyond their final offers by the mediator floating a figure that is tantalisingly close, with all the benefits of settlement coming with it. Or, they might not. £55,000 and £30,000 were both final offers, and you had to work hard to get the parties there. There might be no more movement to come.

And that's where we'll leave this mediation for now, a legal probability wave suspended between a deal and no deal. A lot went well. You empathised and built trust. The parties were advised (had already been advised, in fact) that they faced a degree of risk, they accepted that, and you were able to reframe the mediation in terms of that risk and the value each side put on it. With the Claimant you were also able to reframe the mediation in terms of the consequences of different outcomes: the Defendant was pretty much there already, pitching offers expressly on the basis that he needed the mediation out of the way to focus on other things. All of that generated movement. Maybe enough. Maybe not. The outcome is probably too close to call.

But I think there's more we could have done.

You won't have forgotten that at the end of the last chapter I said that litigants often seem to have a blind spot for the potential downsides of the litigation until they are brought home to them by the mediator, and that it's when they see those downsides clearly that their loss aversion will really kick in. That's what else we could have done, and that's what could have turned a mediation that now hangs suspended between a deal and no deal into one where the parties are shaking hands on a settlement. And that's what you would have done. You would have helped them to get over that blind spot.

I said in the Introduction to this book that this was a book about something magical. I'll bet that you thought that was just a figure of speech. Well, maybe so. But maybe not. Decide for yourselves. Because if there's anything in this book that is magical, that can turn a mediation that doesn't settle into one that does, well, this is it…

Something magical (2)

Let's start with the Claimant. He was advised that his chances of success were 60 to 70%.

His first aspiration as to a settlement figure was based on that 70% chance (He hoped to settle for £70,000 plus £5,000 costs = £75,000, though he opened with an offer of £85,000 to give himself "wiggle room").

Next, when he saw that neither £85,000 nor £75,000 was remotely realistic in the context of the negotiation, he moved to the lower end of the percentage scale his advisor had given him: 60% (leading to an offer of £60,000 plus £5,000 costs = £65,000).

His final position was to ignore the percentage assessments in his legal advice entirely, perhaps because of his intuitive knowledge that all advice about litigation is ultimately unreliable, perhaps driven by risk aversion, and offer to accept a 50/50 split: £50,000 plus £5,000 costs = £55,000.

All reasonable positions. A mediator often sees those. Start at the higher end of the range your legal advisor has given, then try the lower end of the range, and finally there's simply a figure that you'll go to just to get a settlement, in this case meeting in the middle.

But here's the thing. All of these figures are based on a scale that runs from £0 at its lowest point to £100,000 at its highest. Which seems fair enough to the Claimant: £100,000 is what he's claiming and is what he wins if successful and £0 is what he gets if he loses. So, that's his scale: £0 to £100,000. 70% equates to £70,000, 60% to £60,000 and meeting in the middle means £50,000 (to each of which figures the Claimant added £5,000 for his costs). All fine and dandy, except that in the real world – the world of the First Noble Truth, the one that isn't as we'd like it to be – the possible outcomes for the Claimant aren't poised between £0 and £100,000 at all.

If the Claimant wins, he recovers £100,000, for sure (assuming the Defendant company is good for the money). But, he also spends another £50,000 on top of what he's already spent in legal costs, and we know that he'll probably only recover 60% of that, so £30,000. Which means that if the Claimant wins, he's actually £80,000 better off (£100,000 - £50,000 + £30,000) not £100,000 better off.

It gets worse. If he loses, he still has to pay his own legal costs: £50,000. Plus, he has to pay 60% of the Defendant's costs of £50,000, which is another £30,000. Losing will cost him £50,000 + £30,000 = £80,000.

And there you have it. The Claimant – and I see this in so many mediations – for all his awareness of the risk, for all his risk aversion – appears to have had a blind spot for the potential downsides of the litigation. He's only really looking at the prize of winning of £100,000, and that determined his negotiating posture. His percentages and his assessments are all based on a scale running from £0 to £100,000. As a result, and risk averse though he is, he might just be about to walk away from a deal at anything less than £50,000 or maybe even £55,000.

But in fact, he stands poised between winning £80,000…. *and losing £80,000*. It's exactly the same win / lose scenario that we saw when we looked at Kahneman and Tversky's work in Chapter 5 (see; I told you the figures of £8 / £80 / £800 / £8,000 / £80,000 etc weren't random) and we saw then that if people are offered a prize of £80,000 if they win, but have to pay £80,000 if they lose, risk aversion is such that most people don't want to take the risk. They'd rather hold what they have. Even if their chances are better than even, if £80,000 is more than they can comfortably lose, they'd rather not run the risk. Businesses may be a bit less risk averse than individuals, yes, but the Claimant's business is a small family business and losing £80,000 is almost certainly more than he can afford to lose, so that's not going to be a risk he's comfortable taking.

And just to be clear, it's not that the Claimant hasn't been advised of the chances of success or the costs consequences of winning or losing. As I said earlier, I find that most of the lawyers I mediate are great in the advice they give about the risks, and the upside and downside of litigation, and we can safely assume that the Claimant knows all this. At one level. It's just that there can be a blind spot for the downsides until they're brought to the fore. The Claimant knows it, but he doesn't quite see it.

Which is partly why I often use a flip chart to highlight the upside and the downsides of litigation. I like flip charts. In a mediation I mean, I wouldn't want to go on holiday with one or have several in each room at home. But in a mediation I like them. A lot. They have several advantages. Firstly, I'm definitely a stupid bear when it comes to figures, my maths can be a bit rubbish, and if I write the figures up on a flip chart, the parties to the dispute or their numerically gifted lawyers can correct any mathematical howlers. And that's great, because it makes the figures we're writing up a common endeavour, not my figures imposed on the parties, and if the figures are the result of a common endeavour the parties are much more likely to buy into them (which doesn't mean that I make the mistakes deliberately, the great thing about my mistakes is that they happen all on their own). Secondly, I have a theory, for which I have no evidence or authority at all, except that it seems to be borne out by my experience, that the mere act of lifting one's head to look at the figures on a flip chart loosens the muscles in the back of the neck thereby releasing tension, and generally making people feel more optimistic, more capable of making a move, and less stuck. I lift up mine eyes to thy hills, O Lord, wrote the psalmist. If there's a psalm about lifting up mine eyes to thy flipchart, O mediator, I'm afraid it's passed me by, but getting people to physically lift up their eyes to a flipchart, if not quite inspiring a religious experience, simply seems to create a more positive, flexible mood in a mediation. And most importantly, the mediator's role, having empathised and won the parties' trust, is to help them reframe the litigation in terms of risk and reward and, when you think about it, writing the possible outcomes up on a flipchart in financial terms is pretty much the ultimate act of reframing. Have a look at this…

In our mediation, the Claimant had begun by framing this dispute in terms of the *high quality* of his widgets, the *great expertise* that he has as a member of the National Institute of Widget Makers (West Midlands Region), and his lawyer added to that the *legal correctness* of his position. There's absolutely no point challenging that narrative by slapping him round the face with the wet fish of the Defendant's case, because there's simply no possibility of the Claimant adopting a narrative that says his widgets were rubbish, actually, that he's a one-man band who doesn't know what he's doing, and neither do the National Institute of Widget Makers (West Midlands Region) and that on top of all that his legal position is up the spout. But reframed on a flip chart as a Risk / Reward proposition – using (and this is crucial) the figures and percentages that have come from his own lawyer about possible outcomes and their costs consequences – that narrative about *quality*, *expertise* and *correctness* disappears, or rather, is reframed to look like something like this:

WIN	LOSE
Recover £100,000 damages	Recover £0 damages
Pay £50,000 own legal costs	Pay £50,000 own legal costs
Recover £30,000 costs contribution	Pay £30,000 costs contribution
Net position: +£80,000	Net position: -£80,000
60 / 70% chance of winning £80,000	*30 / 40% chance of losing £80,000*

Looks a bit different, doesn't it? All those value judgements about the quality of the widgets and the Claimant's expertise in widgets, all the legal arguments, all of which would have hemmed in the Claimant's ability to move are gone, replaced by financial outcomes and by percentages as to the chances of each occurring in the less than perfect world of the First Noble Truth. And the great thing about the figures is that (a) as we've said, they've come from the Claimant's own side, from him or his lawyer, and (b) they're just figures. Figures don't come with a moral charge, and so figures permit movement without having to compromise one's moral position. What's more, they shine a great big shiny light on that blind spot that the Claimant – for all his risk aversion – had about the downsides of the litigation. There's a chance, a chance that might be as high as 40%, that this litigation ends with the Claimant losing £80,000.

I once did a similar exercise for a businessman from just outside London, running a business not totally unlike that of the Claimant, on figures not a million miles from these, after he had explained to me his willingness to be reasonable but also his determination to litigate if settlement terms that recognised the *moral correctness* and *legal strength* of his case weren't met. After reframing the litigation, with his solicitors' figures, as a risk / reward proposition in this way on a flip chart, I said that I needed to go and spend a little time with the other side, and invited him and his lawyer to consider what was on the flipchart. When I came back, he'd turned the flipchart round to face the wall. "I can't bear to look at it", he said "it's just obvious, isn't it? You've got to get me out of this litigation, Martin, just get me out of it".

I'm guessing that once our mild mannered Claimant had seen his claim rephrased as a 60 to 70% chance of winning £80,000 and a 30 to 40% chance of losing £80,000, he'd have ended up in pretty much the same position, namely that he would have wanted to get out of a piece of litigation that had suddenly lost its allure on pretty much the best available terms. You'd have to have carried out this exercise with him at the point where you'd won his trust (no point doing it earlier!), when the advice about his chances of winning (and, therefore, of losing) is out in the open, but before the first proposals are put. The Three Offer

Rule (Extended Version) tells us that the jumps between the offers the parties to a dispute make never get bigger, and that seems to hold true even if there's some clever reframing on a flipchart part way through the process of making offers. Perhaps that's surprising. You'd think that even if the litigation is reframed in these terms at a late stage in the negotiating process, say when final offers are about to be made, that once the downsides are dragged kicking and screaming from behind the blind spot that they were hiding behind, they'd still have maximum effect and generate a big jump at the last. Well, perhaps you wouldn't have thought that, dear reader. But I would. I did, in fact. And I was wrong. I have to report that the jumps between the different phases of the Three Offer Rule (Extended Version) still don't get bigger. I don't know why. It must be something to do with how our brains are wired. But it's true, I promise you.

So, you need to help the Claimant by reframing the dispute in these terms, and bringing the downside into focus before the first offer is made. And I'm pretty confident that his negotiating proposals would have been markedly different if he's looking at a 30 to 40% chance of losing £80,000, which is more than he's comfortable losing. Believing that he has a claim for £100,000, and a downside that he might recover £0, one can more or less see why he might open the bidding, as it were, with the figure of £85,000. But seeing that he's actually poised between winning £80,000 and losing £80,000, I'm guessing that he wouldn't even have opened at the figure of £85,000 which actually represents more than his best-case outcome. Most people don't need telling that they're not going to settle litigation on terms that are better than their best case if they go to court! Nor would he have fixated on "meeting in the middle", since the midpoint between +£80,000 and -£80,000 is a great big fat zero. Where would he have opened the bidding? I don't know. It's not a real mediation, remember, I'm making this up, and your guess is as good as mine. I'm guessing he might have opened at £60,000 (perhaps with costs, perhaps inclusive of costs) then maybe dropped to £50,000 or even £40,000 and maybe his final offer might have been £30,000. £30,000 doesn't look so bad when compared against a scale that runs from -£80,000 to +£80,000: in fact it's 62.5% of the way along a scale that starts from -£80,000 and runs to

+£80,000, and so absolutely consistent with settling on the basis of the legal advice he received that he had a 60 to 70% chance of winning. You might even point that out to him and his solicitor, though whether you do that would be a bit of a judgement call, because doing that might just come across a bit like the mediator being clever. And there's no place in mediation for the mediator being clever (which may explain why – apparently – I've proved reasonably good at it). Plus, if the Claimant could see his way to accepting £30,000 without your pointing it out then there's no need anyway. £30,000, remember, was the figure that the Defendant was prepared to offer.

But, actually, it's better than that. The Defendant was prepared to offer £30,000 *before* we got round to shining a light on his blind spot about the downsides for him. As mediators, we stand or fall by our impartiality, and we wouldn't do this exercise with the Claimant without replicating it with the Defendant, from his point of view. And, yes, the Defendant has a whopping great big blind spot all of his own. The scale of outcomes he's using when he makes his first offer also runs from £0 to £100,000, though in his case £0 is what he perceives as his best case – not paying the Claimant anything – and £100,000 is what he perceives as his worst case: the sum to be paid to the Claimant if he were to lose. That first offer – £0 – is made at his extreme best case end of that scale.

In fact, in terms of what this litigation is going to cost him, the scale doesn't start at £0. He, or rather, the Defendant company, is going to be £20,000 out of pocket in terms of his unrecoverable legal costs even if he wins – something he is half aware of, being a commercial man, because it surfaces as the rationale for his second offer (£20,000), though it was absent from his deliberations when he made his first offer. And, of course, if he were to lose, this dispute costs him a lot more than the £100,000 he has to pay the Claimant. There's the £100,000 the Defendant would have to pay the Claimant, plus the £50,000 he'd spend on his own costs, plus the £30,000 he'd have to contribute to the Claimant's costs. Reframed in these terms, using the numbers and the risk assessment percentages provided by his own lawyers, the Defendant's own risk / reward equation looks like this:

WIN	LOSE
Pay £0 damages Pay £50,000 own legal costs Recover £30,000 costs contribution Net position: -£20,000	Pay £100,000 damages Pay £50,000 own legal costs Pay £30,000 costs contribution Net position: -£180,000
70 / 80% chance of spending £20,000	*20 / 30% chance of spending £180,000*

Once again, reframed like this, with the value judgements stripped out of it, the downsides loom rather larger than when the dispute is framed in terms of whose expert is the member of the more prestigious trade association. That scale from £0 to £100,000 turns out to have missed the downsides of both a successful and an unsuccessful outcome. At best, it's going to cost the Defendant, £20,000, at worst, £180,000. And that would probably be enough. Faced with those figures on a flipchart I doubt the Defendant would open the bidding at £0. After all, he's a commercial man. A very commercial man. And the proposition that as MD he wouldn't spend a single penny to buy off a 20 / 30% risk of having to pay out £180,000 wouldn't look, well, wouldn't look very commercial. I'm guessing that he'd start at £20,000 and move up from there, and I'm pretty confident that if necessary he'd go above the £30,000 figure which he stopped at when the downsides of the litigation were hidden behind that blind spot.

You might even tweak the reframing of the litigation by asking the Defendant's MD the rhetorical question as to whether he adds value to the business? Of course he does! And your follow-up question would then be to ask him to put a figure on how much value will be taken out of the business if their time and attention is wasted by dealing with this claim. This is a technique I use sparingly: it can look as if the mediator is trying to manipulate the parties in a particular direction. But, where the individual conducting the negotiation plainly puts a high price on their own time I think it's sometimes legitimate. In each case, it's a judgement call, and my instinct is that you wouldn't do it with the Claimant – he is what the Defendant undiplomatically calls a "one-man band" and the risk is that his answer would be that he'll just work nights and weekends to make up the time, because this business is his life, so that there's no cost to the business of the time that the litigation will take up, and that answer won't help, and may even hinder the settlement process. But the Defendant – or rather, the Defendant's MD – has spent the mediation telling you about his all round commercial excellence, and so you might make the call to ask him. And if he thought, say, that his time is so valuable that this litigation will take at least £20,000 in value out of the business, win or lose, then his flip chart could be amended to look like this:

WIN	LOSE
Pay £0 damages	Pay £100,000 damages
Pay £50,000 own legal costs	Pay £50,000 own legal costs
Recover £30,000 costs contribution	Pay £30,000 costs contribution
Value of MD's time: £20,000	Value of MD's time: £20,000
Net position: -£40,000	Net position: -£200,000
70 / 80% chance of spending £40,000	*20 / 30% chance of spending £200,000*

And if the Defendant comes to see that the scale of outcomes in this litigation is not from £0 to £100,000, not even from -£20,000 to -£180,000 but actually from -£40,000 to -£200,000 well, he's going to be that much more pleased to get a deal at, say, £40,000 or £45,000. And we're confident that the Claimant will come below that, so there really ought to be a deal.

The Art of Evaluating Risk

There's also a technique to evaluate with mathematical precision the precise value or risk represented by a given claim which you might consider deploying here. Mediation and the Art of Evaluating Risk, if you like. Again, it's a technique I use very sparingly: it can appear as if the mediator is putting their own figure on the settlement value for the dispute. The mediator is doing no such thing, of course, because all the figures one feeds into what is essentially a simple mathematical model come from the parties or their advisors, and the mediator is just drawing out the mathematical consequences of the advice that the parties are receiving. But, that's not the point: it can *look* as if the mediator is coming up with their own figure, and that's a look we never, ever want to allow. On top of which, it's just a bit complicated, and there's a risk that one loses the party one is talking to in the complications. In mediation, simple is good, complicated not so good. Especially when it's me doing the figures! Plus it's a level of complication that's mostly unnecessary, since simply reframing the litigation as a risk / reward proposition in the simple binary way I've done above is usually enough to let the parties find their own way to their own settlement figure, and very probably it would be enough in our mediation. In our mediation you wouldn't have done this exercise with the Claimant, who wore his risk aversion very much on his sleeve and for whom the litigation reframed on his flip chart as a binary representation of winning and losing would look plenty unattractive enough as it is. But there's just a possibility that a commercial man like the Defendant's MD, who prides himself on both his commerciality and his litigation experience, might rather enjoy the exercise of putting a precise figure on the risk presented by the claim. It would be a judgement call, but you might just try this technique. To do that, you'd need firm risk percentages. You could just suggest using the midpoint of the range the Defendant's solicitor has given (making this a 75/25% chance of winning / losing) or you might just ask the Defendant's solicitor which end of his 70/80% range to us: I've never, ever done that without the solicitor saying that we should err on the side of caution[11], which would

---

11 How surprising.

make this a case with a 70/30% chance of winning. The formula for putting a precise figure of risk (in a binary case) is

(% chance of winning x net financial effect of winning)
+ (% chance of losing x net financial effect of losing)

On that basis, the settlement value of this case would be:

(A 70% chance that the case costs £20,000. 70% x £20,000 = £14,000)

+

(A 30% chance that the case costs £180,000. 30% x £180,000 = £54,000)

Giving a commercial settlement value of £14,000 + £54,000 = £68,000.

In other words, if the Defendant litigated this case one hundred times, and won exactly 70 times and lost 30 times (reflecting exactly the 70% chance of winning) then the average cost to the Defendant of the litigation across the 100 cases would be £68,000 per case. Which means that on a purely actuarial basis one could say that the Defendant would be well advised to consider any settlement at less than £68,000. The technique can be adapted for multiple outcomes by the way: so long as the percentage chances ascribed to each outcome add up to 100, the formula will give an accurate evaluation of the risk posed by the case.

Caveat mediator. Even if the Defendant's MD is up for it and you do frame the case in these terms, as a case with a 70% chance of costing the Defendant £20,000 and a 30% chance of costing the Defendant £180,000 and therefore as a case with a commercial settlement value of up to £68,000, the Defendant's MD isn't going to open the bidding at that figure, and in fact I doubt he'd go to that figure at all. It might, from a strictly mathematical point of view, represent the mathematical risk to the Defendant company, but we're none of us purely mathematical beings. However commercial we might pride ourselves on being. I'm guessing that the figure will just feel too high to the Defendant's

MD. And that's fair enough, because it's arguably a misleading figure *at this point in time* in that it takes into account the ultimate litigation costs, and gives the Claimant the benefit of those in the settlement figure, even though they haven't been incurred yet. It's accurate, but perhaps only at the end of the trial when the judge is about to give judgement and all those cost have been incurred. There again, one could equally argue that from a commercial point of view, if that's what it's ultimately going to cost the Defendant company if they don't settle it, then the commercial thing to do would be to take the actual final cost into account, and that any deal at a lesser figure might be worth considering. And that's really the point of the exercise: not to get the Defendant to offer £68,000, but to give him permission, if you like, to view a settlement at a lower figure as a sensible and, yes, commercial decision. Once the MD has seen a calculation that values the risk posed by this claim at £68,000 he will probably feel mightily pleased with himself if he can settle this for a figure in the region of £30,000 / £40,000 / £45,000. And we mediators like to please.

But as I say, probably you wouldn't even need to use this technique to put a precise value on the litigation risk. Simply addressing the parties' respective blind spots, reframing the case in terms that brings the potential downside for each party into focus, is likely to be enough.

At what figure does it settle? I don't know. That's not our job to say. I could write up an account of the conclusion of this imaginary mediation, once the parties have both seen past the blind spot that they had for the downsides, and pick a figure. Maybe somewhere around £40,000? Maybe more. Or less. Since this mediation is made up from start to finish, my picking a figure and telling you what it was wouldn't prove anything, and might give credence to the myth that the mediator has a figure or an outcome in mind for every mediation, a figure that is the *right* outcome. And rather like all those other value judgements that we spent time reframing in the mediation in order to help the parties move away from, the notion of a *right* outcome is just another set of words imposed upon the shifting cinders of the world. If you subscribe to a belief in absolute goodness, or in a Creator of the Universe who takes a personal interest in the outcome of your mediations then, maybe, there is a *right* outcome. Maybe there isn't. But we flawed human beings aren't so good at seeing ultimate values, which means that in mediation the right outcome is simply the one to which the parties find their own way.

Zen Mediation

So, there you go. Zen mediation. Or, if you like, mediation based on principles derived from the Buddha's Noble Truths, as those Noble Truths appear to a practising mediator. Recognise that people aren't happy about being in dispute. Affirm and build trust. Don't try to slap people around the face with a wet fish. Help them to come to terms with the potentially unsatisfactory and definitely risky outcome of litigation in an imperfect world. Let them see the downsides of litigation, as well as the potential gains. And then help them to negotiate a deal that isn't perfect either, but which is certain, and which they might prefer to the uncertainty of the litigation. Easy, really. Obvious, actually. So obvious that I wouldn't have bothered to write this book at all, except that there's so many mediators out there doing something altogether different. And I've seen them doing it, and it's not pretty. Stand up and take a bow, Humphrey Forbes-Smythe QC. And do you have to practice Zen, or be any kind of Buddhist, to mediate in the way I've described? No, no and three times no. I make that five "no's" in all, but if you'd like some more, feel free to add them. The thing about the Noble Truths is, they're just, well, true. And truth doesn't come with an agenda to promote Zen Buddhism. Truth doesn't care tuppence about Zen Buddhism. Truth is non-denominational. If a spiritual teacher pronounced that the sun rises in the east and sets in the west, that wouldn't make this insight the property of that teacher or their followers. And the insight that litigants are dissatisfied about being in litigation and stuck as a result, and that the way to unstick them is to win their trust and then help them come to terms with their situation, well, that's about as obvious as the one about where the sun rises and sets. I experience it, and express it, in terms of the Buddha's Noble Truths because Zen Buddhism happens to be my path. But you can express it in your terms. That's fine. Your terms will work better for you. Your mediation practice, your path.

And if all this sounds like I'm winding up to a conclusion to this little book, well, I'm not. Not yet, anyway. As you'll know if you know anything at all about Buddhism beyond the fact that the Buddha is the fat laughing guy, there are not three, but four Noble Truths. So we've got one more Noble Truth to go. Read on, to discover the Final Noble Truth…

CHAPTER SEVEN

The Fourth Noble Truth

The Buddha liked lists. The Three Jewels.[1] The Four Noble Truths. The Five Precepts.[2] And so on. There are even Buddhist scholars who have compiled lists of the Buddha's lists. So perhaps I should have been prepared, but even so I confess that I was just a bit surprised when, in the early stages of my journey into Zen Buddhism, I reached the last of the Buddha's Four Noble Truths only to find that it turns out to be, yes, another list.

I guess the problem is that my expectations have been shaped by "Western"[3] stories or myths, as seen through the lens of Hollywood. And as a result, I was, perhaps subconsciously, rather expecting the Final Truth to be something a little more, well, a little more impressive, a little more *final*. In Hollywood films, Final Truths tend to be impressive. If Indiana Jones had leapt out of all those moving vehicles, battled snakes and escaped from Nazis only to find that the Holy Grail was actually a shopping list, it would have been something of an anticlimax, and there wouldn't have been all those sequels. And I suppose that, perhaps subconsciously, I expected something more from the Buddha's Final Truth. Find the Buddha Grail, my child, the Grail from which the Buddha himself drank on the day of his death, dip it thrice in the sacred waters of the Buddha stream, the stream in which the Buddha himself bathed, then drink reverently from the Grail itself and if your heart is pure you will ever after be able to eat unlimited carbohydrates. That kind of thing.

---

1 The Buddha, the Dharma (teaching) and the Sangha (community), since you didn't ask.

2 Don't kill, steal, hurt through sex, lie or otherwise speak hurtfully, or consume alcohol so as to lose your faculties (unless it's Friday evening and it's been a really bad week).

3 "Western"? Rather depends where you're standing, surely?

In a way, the Buddha's Final Truth is that there isn't a Final Truth. Now, before the Buddha Police jump on me and cart me off to Buddha School for Remedial Buddha Study, yes, I know that's not technically correct. If you ever need to impress anyone with your knowledge of Buddhism, then technically the Fourth Noble Truth is that the Path to Enlightenment is the Noble Eightfold Path. And if you want to know what that is (and even if you don't want to know) the Noble Eightfold Path (which has been variously translated) may for our purposes be said to be: appropriate speech, appropriate actions, an appropriate livelihood, appropriate mindfulness, appropriate meditation, an appropriate resolve, an appropriate effort, and an appropriate view. That's an appropriate view as in an appropriate understanding of how the world really is, not as in a nice view when you look out of the window. Though maybe that could help too. But my point is that the Buddha's Final Truth is that there's no one easy answer, no Buddha Grail: you're going to have to work on these eight areas of your life. And, guess what: when it comes to each area, there's usually another list. Appropriate speech, for example involves: not lying, not speaking hurtfully, not gossiping, and only saying what is helpful. Drill down into any element of the Noble Eightfold Path and you'll see that it subdivides into more things to work on. Rather like the delta of a mighty river like the Nile, the Buddha's Fourth Noble Truth keeps subdividing and subdividing until it has irrigated every aspect of your life. And if I was briefly disappointed to find that the Buddha's Final Truth wasn't some one-shot-fixes-everything Budhha Grail, I've come to feel that actually, the Buddha's Final Truth was just what the Final Truth – any Final Truth, or at least any Final Truth that's actually, well, *true* – had to be. There is no Buddha Grail. You want to fix your life? You're going to have to work on your life. Yes, all of it. D'oh!

You may think that's ultimately pretty obvious. Again, as with most of the Buddha's truths. You may think that what's really a universal truth was never going to be hidden in a box somewhere waiting for Indiana Jones to discover it, because that wouldn't be a universal truth, that would be a small fits-in-a-box sized thing hidden in a box. You may think that anything that's really a universal truth is probably out-of-the-box-staring-you-in-the-face, there-all-the-time obvious because, well, because it's (a) universal, and (b) true. Zen Master Dogen (whose Rules for Meditation we encountered in chapter three) said precisely that:

> "*The Truth is universal. The truth is not far away. By its very nature, the Truth is ever present. The Truth is always here.*"

But just because the Fourth Noble Truth may – once you know it – be obvious, that doesn't mean it's easy. Finding the Buddha Grail would have been altogether easier. The Fourth Noble Truth requires unremitting effort, working on the Noble Eightfold Path across all aspects of your life. And that work is never done. Zen Buddhists may take four vows:

Beings are numberless. I vow to save them all.

Ignorance is inexhaustible. I vow to end it.

The Dharma[4] is boundless. I vow to master it.

The Buddha Way is unattainable. I vow to attain it.

Tough, hey? Beings are numberless, so you're not going to be able to save them all. Obviously. Nor end what is inexhaustible. Nor master what is boundless. Nor attain the unattainable. Which, depending on your point of view, is either setting you up for an awful lot of falls, or incredibly liberating, since the moment you make the vows, you're on the path and doing what you can. In Zen, that's all one can do: make the vows, and keep on trying. Zen is a path, not a goal. And practising is the path.

And if you were hoping, dear reader, that this little chapter was going to reveal the Final Truth about Mediation, the location of the Mediator's Grail, drinking from which will instantly make you a successful and effective mediator, then I'm afraid that I'm going to disappoint you. There is no Mediator's Grail. Sorry about that. The First, Second and Third Noble Truths of Mediation have taught us that as mediators we offer affirmation and empathy in the face of people's dissatisfaction

---

4 The teaching of the Buddha and those that followed him

with their situation, we recognise the value judgement laden narratives that run in their minds, and we help them to reframe those mental narrative in a way that allows them to move their position. The Fourth Noble Truth of Mediation is simply that we're going to have to work on this stuff. On our mediation technique, yes. As importantly, perhaps more importantly, we can develop the mindset, the empathy, the understanding and the compassion that empowers those techniques, which is really what this book has also been about. If the empathy, the understanding and the compassion are there, good mediation technique comes without thinking about it, and when deployed, it'll be powerful and move people. Either way, no, we won't reach perfection as mediators. But so long as we're working on it, every mediation, every time, we're on the path.

The goalless goal

What's more, in Zen Buddhism being on the path is the only place we could be. Not only will we not reach perfection, but what's perfection? Isn't that just another word, another subjective value judgement that ultimately has no grounding in reality? Finally – *finally* – Norwich City scored the perfect goal last weekend. Yes, really. A beautiful curling strike into the top corner of the opposition net. The boys in yellow and green don't score perfect goals very often. In fact, right now as I write this, they don't score goals of any kind very often: period. So I think I know the perfect Norwich City goal when I see one. Except, it wasn't the perfect goal if you had the misfortune to be a fan of the opposition. It was a fluke, a lucky long shot that was only possible because of a defensive blunder in the first place. That's the trouble with perfection. It's in the eye of the beholder. A concept in the mind, a story we tell ourselves. That's all.

And if you're trying to reach the goal of perfection, in your Zen practice or your mediation practice, or in anything else come to that, then, when you think about it, you're telling yourself a story about how the world *should* be, and wanting the world to conform to that story. "I *should* be able to perfect my meditation technique / mediation technique / recipe for low carb moussaka, but I can't! If *only* I could sit in the full lotus position for an hour[5] / could improve my reframing technique / could find a low carb alternative for potatoes in the moussaka[6] then my Zen practice / mediation practice / low carb moussaka would be perfect and everything would be cool". Except that, sorry, but it wouldn't. Something else would nag at you, and someone would disagree, and someone else would say that actually it wasn't the potatoes in the moussaka, it was carbohydrates in the tomatoes that were the problem all along. The problem with the goal of reaching perfection, or enlightenment, or whatever floats your boat, is that you won't get there (and if you did it wouldn't be what you thought it would be) and that in the meantime you won't be as effective, whether in your Zen practice, or in your work as a mediator, or indeed in any aspect of your life, because your focus won't be on what you're doing. It will be on that illusory goal, on the story you tell yourself about how your world should be. There's a story about a student who asked a Zen Master how long he would have to practice in order to attain a degree of enlightenment. "Ten years," replied the Zen Master. "Ah", said the student, but what if I practice twice as hard, how quickly will I attain enlightenment then?" "Twenty years," replied the Zen Master. "How can that be?" asked the student. The Zen Master replied: "When you always have one eye on the goal, you can only have one eye on the path".

Up to this point we've focussed on how the Four Noble Truths apply to the parties to a dispute. And we've discussed how the mediator's role is to help the parties free themselves from the stories that they've told themselves about how their dispute should be resolved. But here's the thing, and perhaps this is a Final Mediation Truth after all: the Four Noble Truths apply to mediators as much as the next person. Truth is a bit like that, it has this habit of applying across the board. I've observed plenty of mediators in action (including, if you'll permit some self-reflection, myself). We're not satisfied with the world as we find it, either, and we tell ourselves stories about how the world should be and

---

5   Ouch. Do not try this at home. Actually, do not try this at all.

6   Just leave the potatoes out. Maybe up the aubergines a bit. It'll be fine. Moussaka doesn't need potatoes. I promise.

specifically about how our mediation practice should be, and how the mediation in front of us should run, and we focus on the fact that neither the world, nor our mediation practice nor the mediation in front of us are as we'd like them to be, as they *should* be, dammit. I've seen mediators who spend almost all their energy during a mediation obsessing over whether that booking for their next mediation has come in or not, checking their mobile phone or laptop between every session. Yes, really. I've seen mediators worrying over whether they're making a good impression on the solicitors present, who might instruct them on further mediations. I've seen mediators worrying over when the mediation is going to finish, and whether they'll make the last train home. Most of all, I've seen mediators stressing over whether the case is going to settle, because they're worried about their settlement rate, or because they think the solicitors involved will never instruct them again if they don't settle this case, or perhaps because they just care and don't want to fail to deliver a settlement for the parties.

Brother and sister mediators, I've been there. I've stressed about where my next mediation booking is coming from (though not actually during a mediation – that was a big name mediator whom I observed mediating long, long ago). But, yes, I've worried about the impression I make on the solicitors who instruct me, because at the end of the day they're the people who send me the work that enables Zaza the Fat Cat to live in the manner to which she has become rather too accustomed. Most of all, though, I've stressed about settling the case I was dealing with at that moment. Because it *should* settle. Because it would be *wrong*, just *wrong*, to spend the money litigating. Because I care about the parties and think settlement would be *best* for them. And as with all the stories we tell ourselves, they didn't make me any happier, and they certainly didn't make me a better mediator. Quite the reverse, actually.

As long as the mediator is listening to their own mental story that the case *must* settle, their effectiveness will be diminished. Partly, perhaps, because they'll be too busy worrying about whether the case is going to settle to really, really pay attention to what's going on in front of them: they won't be there, in the moment with the parties, they'll always have one eye on the goal of settlement. But also because the parties will sense that the mediator is working to an agenda. Which will make them resistant. It's human nature to dig our heels in if we think someone is trying to get us to do something.

More than that, if the mediator has an agenda that the case must settle, that mediator's agenda will take from the client the liberating choice of deciding whether to move on with their own lives or to remain stuck in the dispute, because the mediator has in effect tried to decide for them. But, it's *their* life, *their* dispute, and *their* decision to stay stuck or to move. The gift we mediators give the parties is to give them back control over their lives by handing the decision on settlement back to them. I sometimes think that there's something symbolic about the seating arrangements in court. At the front facing the learned judge are m'learned friends, the top barristers, the QCs. A row behind them sit m'slightly less learned friends, the junior barristers. Behind them, m'friends the solicitors. Behind them, m'not-at-all-learned[7] friends the trainee solicitors. And who's that person right at the back? Oh yes. *That* would be the client. The actual party to the dispute. And if they, the client, want to communicate something to the judge they write a note. And tap the trainee solicitor on the back. Eventually, they get the trainee's attention and the process is repeated as the note goes forward. From the trainee solicitor to the solicitor. From the solicitor to the junior barrister. And eventually, the junior barrister manages to get the attention of the QC. By which time, the trial has moved beyond the point, and the great man or woman glances briefly at the note before screwing it into a ball and tossing it aside. It's no surprise that the clients report feeling that once they start the litigation process they are out of control, clinging on for dear life to a roller coaster hurtling towards a trial that they couldn't stop if they wanted to. But in a mediation, the mediator sits down with the client and hands the decision back to *them*, and with it, returns to them control of their own life.

Zen masters often refer to Zen practice as the goalless goal. Goalless because there *is* no goal. A goal would just be another story to tell ourselves. We're on the path, practising Zen, working on our lives, and that's all there is. So too with mediation. As mediators, we're on the

---

7 Despite being the holders of a degree in law and a student debt to go with it.

path, practising mediation. We're offering affirmation, building trust, helping to reframe the parties' mental narrative so as to give them the opportunity to unstick their lives and accept a world – and a settlement – that isn't as they would like it to be, if that's what they choose to do. And that's all there is. And here's a bit more magic: it can be the realisation that the mediator is goalless that finally cracks a deadlocked mediation. So long as the mediator has an agenda to settle, they haven't really handed the decision back to the parties to the dispute. And each party may sit back and tell the mediator that the deal isn't good enough, that the mediator hasn't done enough. In effect the parties keep handing the dispute back to the mediator who appears to want to settle it so much. But at the moment where the disputants sense that the mediator has no goal, that this is the deal that's available, and it's the only deal that's available because that's just how the world is, and that the decision whether to accept the world as it is and move on, or not, is theirs and theirs alone, *that* is the moment when the parties to the dispute take back control of their lives and, more often than not, make that final move.

That's the gift the mediator gives the parties to a dispute. We return to them control over their lives. That is the mediator's calling.

How many disputes have I mediated? I don't know. Honestly. Well over a thousand, but I don't know the exact number.

And how many of those thousand plus disputes did I settle?

Now, that number I do know.

None of them.

Not one.

But the parties to those disputes: *they* settled nearly all of them.

APPENDIX
TOP TEN MISTAKES TO AVOID FOR MEDIATORS

We can all learn from each other's experiences. Especially, perhaps, from the mistakes others made. In mediation, however, we don't often get that opportunity, because generally speaking whilst mediators are happy to share details of their successes, they're not so willing to say anything about their mistakes.

But, you've stuck with me to the end, dear reader. I'm grateful. So you deserve something in return, and as a thank you I thought I'd share with you my Top Ten Mistakes to Avoid for Mediators, in the hope that by sharing some of the painful errors that I've made along the Mediator's path I may spare you some of the resultant pain…

1. An efficient booking system is a necessity for a successful mediator's practice. But, next year, and every subsequent year, I shall book out Karen's birthday right at the start of the year. And you, brother and sister mediators, should do the same. Better still, rather than booking out Karen's birthday, book out your own spouse's or significant other's birthday. If you don't, someone is bound to book that day for a mediation on the other side of the country, and that mediation is certain to last until midnight. Which you do not want on that day of all days. Trust me on this.

2. In those cases where the parties must be kept apart at all costs, where even a chance meeting on arrival or on the way to the loo runs the risk that they come to blows, it can sometimes be a good idea to use two completely separate buildings, placing one party in each, if you have access to adjacent or nearby buildings. However, if you do this, and if the mediation is likely to run late, make sure you have a key to both buildings. Mediation

works best when the mediator is not locked out and does not have to climb back in through a first floor window.

3. The parties are entitled to expect you to have read the mediation bundle in an atmosphere conducive to calm concentration. Do not attempt to read the bundle in the presence of a cat. Not even a placid fat one. It will sit on the expert's report, and then spill tea over the position statements.

4. Do not attempt to read the mediation bundle on a train either. Even if there is no cat on the train. Under railway by-laws all lever arch folders and ring binders are now booby-trapped to spring open if removed from a briefcase on a train, distributing the papers over the railway carriage in a most entertaining manner that really does not sit well with the confidentiality of the mediation process.

5. The mediator must go where the dispute is. Which means mediation is a chance to visit and learn to appreciate some of the (inexplicably) lesser known attractions of our sceptered isle. In recent months I have stayed in the exotic luxury of the Balsall Common Premier Inn, the Basildon Rayleigh Premier Inn and the Ware Premier Inn. I have also discovered that Newcastle under Lyme and Newcastle upon Tyne are not the same place. They are not even close. Booking a Premier Inn in one, when your mediation is in the other, is not recommended.

6. If Norwich City (or, should you be unfortunate enough to support another football team, then that team) are playing at home in the evening, the mediation will run late. Too late for you to get to the match. There is nothing you can do about this. Saying "Come on people, we have to settle this, the match is kicking off soon" simply does not work. So you may as well accept it. If you support Norwich City you may take some consolation from the fact that they only ever win when you're not watching, so perhaps without you there they will win.

7. One of the advantages of mediation is the flexibility of the procedure. Nevertheless, even if the case is about them, animals are best left at home. And whatever your views on the controversial question of joint sessions, never, ever try to hold a joint session with animals present.

8. Props can be really useful in mediation. I've sometimes found it useful to put an old bullet on the table in the middle of a mediation, when asking the parties if they have any "golden bullets" in the way of legal points to fire: it raises a smile, and breaks the tension all round. But if you're flying to the mediation venue, as I quite often do from Norwich's excellent airport, do not take the bullet with you in your suit pocket. The scanner thing you have to walk through will go off, and a lot of charming heavily armed people will appear and want to know why you are boarding the plane with a bullet, Sir, and it all just gets complicated. Leave the bullet at home.

9. Mediation can settle the most unlikely cases. So you should on no account, ever, say to the parties: "If this case settles I will run naked around Norwich Cathedral at midday". Do not even think about it.

10. Following on from 9, above, never make the mistake of giving up hope. Not in your career as a mediator, nor in the mediation process in general, nor in the prospects of a particular case settling. Despite the cats, the exploding ring binders, the location of Newcastle under Lyme, and the other challenges that beset us, the overwhelming majority of cases do settle. Mediation works. I'm not sure I understand fully why it works so well, and in part this book has been an attempt to answer that question for myself. But the fact remains: mediation just works. Have faith. Good luck!

ACKNOWLEDGMENTS

I have been so lucky in life, and I owe thanks to so many people who have helped me along the way generally, and specifically in the production of this book, that I can't possibly mention them all, but my thanks are due in particular: to every lawyer and to every client who has ever instructed me to mediate – each mediation was a privilege and it is literally true to say that without you, this book would never have been written; to the Mediation Police, that is to say, to everyone at the Civil Mediation Council and to everyone else who counts as part of the great and the good of the mediation establishment – without you, the profession that it has been my privilege to follow wouldn't exist, and I love you all really; to my old friend Roger, who was the first person to believe in this book; to Clare and Judith, who read it and ever so tactfully pointed out bits that I might want to have a second look at; to my colleagues at mediation1st, especially Mandy and Susan – the crème de la crème of mediation; to my mum, who died whilst I was writing this book, who first taught me that conflict is never the answer, and that understanding another's perspective usually is; to my children Tom, James and Joss – there is probably nothing that teaches one more about human nature than raising children and it has been my privilege to be your father and I'm so proud of each of you; and most of all to my wife Karen, my friend, my companion, and the love of my life, who has caused me to doubt the First Noble Truth.

MORE BOOKS BY
LAW BRIEF PUBLISHING

A selection of our other titles available now:-

'A Practical Guide to the SRA Principles, Individual and Law Firm Codes of Conduct 2019 – What Every Law Firm Needs to Know' by Paul Bennett
'A Practical Guide to Licensing Law for Commercial Property Lawyers' by Niall McCann & Richard Williams
'A Practical Guide to Adoption for Family Lawyers' by Graham Pegg
'Essential Motor Finance Law for the Busy Practitioner' by Richard Humphreys
'A Practical Guide to Industrial Disease Claims' by Andrew Mckie & Ian Skeate
'Employment Law and the Gig Economy' by Nigel Mackay & Annie Powell
'A Practical Guide to the Law of Armed Conflict' by Jo Morris & Libby Anderson
'A Practical Guide to Redundancy' by Philip Hyland
'A Practical Guide to Vicarious Liability' by Mariel Irvine
'A Practical Guide to Claims Arising from Delays in Diagnosing Cancer' by Bella Webb
'A Practical Guide to Applications for Landlord's Consent and Variation of Leases' by Mark Shelton
'A Practical Guide to Relief from Sanctions Post-Mitchell and Denton' by Peter Causton
'Butler's Equine Tax Planning: 2nd Edition' by Julie Butler
'A Practical Guide to Equity Release for Advisors' by Paul Sams
'A Practical Guide to Immigration Law and Tier 1 Entrepreneur Applications' by Sarah Pinder
'A Practical Guide to Unlawful Eviction and Harassment' by Stephanie Lovegrove
'In My Backyard! A Practical Guide to Neighbourhood Plans' by Dr Sue Chadwick
'A Practical Guide to the Law Relating to Food' by Ian Thomas

'A Practical Guide to the Ending of Assured Shorthold Tenancies' by Elizabeth Dwomoh
'Commercial Mediation – A Practical Guide' by Nick Carr
'A Practical Guide to Financial Services Claims' by Chris Hegarty
'The Law of Houses in Multiple Occupation: A Practical Guide to HMO Proceedings' by Julian Hunt
'A Practical Guide to Unlawful Eviction and Harassment' by Stephanie Lovegrove
'A Practical Guide to Solicitor and Client Costs' by Robin Dunne
'Artificial Intelligence – The Practical Legal Issues' by John Buyers
'A Practical Guide to Wrongful Conception, Wrongful Birth and Wrongful Life Claims' by Rebecca Greenstreet
'Occupiers, Highways and Defective Premises Claims: A Practical Guide Post-Jackson – 2nd Edition' by Andrew Mckie
'A Practical Guide to Financial Ombudsman Service Claims' by Adam Temple & Robert Scrivenor
'A Practical Guide to the Law of Enfranchisement and Lease Extension' by Paul Sams
'A Practical Guide to Marketing for Lawyers – 2nd Edition' by Catherine Bailey & Jennet Ingram
'A Practical Guide to Advising Schools on Employment Law' by Jonathan Holden
'Certificates of Lawful Use and Development: A Guide to Making and Determining Applications' by Bob Mc Geady & Meyric Lewis
'A Practical Guide to the Law of Dilapidations' by Mark Shelton
'A Practical Guide to the 2018 Jackson Personal Injury and Costs Reforms' by Andrew Mckie
'A Guide to Consent in Clinical Negligence Post-Montgomery' by Lauren Sutherland QC
'A Practical Guide to Running Housing Disrepair and Cavity Wall Claims: 2nd Edition' by Andrew Mckie & Ian Skeate
'A Practical Guide to the General Data Protection Regulation (GDPR)' by Keith Markham
'A Practical Guide to Digital and Social Media Law for Lawyers' by Sherree Westell

'A Practical Guide to Holiday Sickness Claims – 2nd Edition' by Andrew Mckie & Ian Skeate
'A Practical Guide to Inheritance Act Claims by Adult Children Post-Ilott v Blue Cross' by Sheila Hamilton Macdonald
'A Practical Guide to Elderly Law' by Justin Patten
'Arguments and Tactics for Personal Injury and Clinical Negligence Claims' by Dorian Williams
'A Practical Guide to QOCS and Fundamental Dishonesty' by James Bentley
'A Practical Guide to Drone Law' by Rufus Ballaster, Andrew Firman, Eleanor Clot
'Practical Mediation: A Guide for Mediators, Advocates, Advisers, Lawyers, and Students in Civil, Commercial, Business, Property, Workplace, and Employment Cases' by Jonathan Dingle with John Sephton
'Practical Horse Law: A Guide for Owners and Riders' by Brenda Gilligan
'A Comparative Guide to Standard Form Construction and Engineering Contracts' by Jon Close
'A Practical Guide to Compliance for Personal Injury Firms Working With Claims Management Companies' by Paul Bennett
'A Practical Guide to the Landlord and Tenant Act 1954: Commercial Tenancies' by Richard Hayes & David Sawtell
'A Practical Guide to Personal Injury Claims Involving Animals' by Jonathan Hand
'A Practical Guide to Psychiatric Claims in Personal Injury' by Liam Ryan
'Introduction to the Law of Community Care in England and Wales' by Alan Robinson
'A Practical Guide to Dog Law for Owners and Others' by Andrea Pitt
'Ellis and Kevan on Credit Hire – 5th Edition' by Aidan Ellis & Tim Kevan
'RTA Allegations of Fraud in a Post-Jackson Era: The Handbook – 2nd Edition' by Andrew Mckie
'RTA Personal Injury Claims: A Practical Guide Post-Jackson' by Andrew Mckie
'On Experts: CPR35 for Lawyers and Experts' by David Boyle
'An Introduction to Personal Injury Law' by David Boyle
'A Practical Guide to Claims Arising From Accidents Abroad and Travel Claims' by Andrew Mckie & Ian Skeate

'A Practical Guide to Cosmetic Surgery Claims' by Dr Victoria Handley
'A Practical Guide to Chronic Pain Claims' by Pankaj Madan
'A Practical Guide to Claims Arising from Fatal Accidents' by James Patience
'A Practical Approach to Clinical Negligence Post-Jackson' by Geoffrey Simpson-Scott
'A Practical Guide to Personal Injury Trusts' by Alan Robinson
'Employers' Liability Claims: A Practical Guide Post-Jackson' by Andrew Mckie
'A Practical Guide to Subtle Brain Injury Claims' by Pankaj Madan
'The Law of Driverless Cars: An Introduction' by Alex Glassbrook
'A Practical Guide to Costs in Personal Injury Cases' by Matthew Hoe
'A Practical Guide to Alternative Dispute Resolution in Personal Injury Claims – Getting the Most Out of ADR Post-Jackson' by Peter Causton, Nichola Evans, James Arrowsmith
'A Practical Guide to Personal Injuries in Sport' by Adam Walker & Patricia Leonard
'The No Nonsense Solicitors' Practice: A Guide To Running Your Firm' by Bettina Brueggemann
'Baby Steps: A Guide to Maternity Leave and Maternity Pay' by Leah Waller
'The Queen's Counsel Lawyer's Omnibus: 20 Years of Cartoons from The Times 1993-2013' by Alex Steuart Williams

These books and more are available to order online direct from the publisher at www.lawbriefpublishing.com, where you can also read free sample chapters. For any queries, contact us on 0844 587 2383 or mail@lawbriefpublishing.com.

Our books are also usually in stock at www.amazon.co.uk with free next day delivery for Prime members, and at good legal bookshops such as Hammicks and Wildy & Sons.

We are regularly launching new books in our series of practical day-to-day practitioners' guides. Visit our website and join our free newsletter to be kept informed and to receive special offers, free chapters, etc.

You can also follow us on Twitter at www.twitter.com/lawbriefpub.

Made in United States
Troutdale, OR
03/21/2025